M-Joy Practically Speaking

M-Joy Practically Speaking
Matrix Energetics and Living Your Infinite Potential

Melissa Joy Jonsson

M-JOY OF BEING, INC.

Published by M-Joy Of Being, Inc.
140 Encinitas Blvd. Ste. 302
Encinitas, CA 92024
© 2013 by Melissa Joy Jonsson
All rights reserved. Printed in the United States of America
18 17 16 15 14   1 2 3 4 5

ISBN (print): 978-0-9915346-0-9

Library of Congress Control Number: 2014904063

Cover illustration by Thomas Hougdahl (with great appreciation)
Cover photograph and permission © Torge Niemann, www .torgeniemann.de

Contents

CONTENTS

Foreword

You hold in your hands a key to opening that most magical and sacred of all spaces, the domain of the heart. Be prepared for magnificence.

Melissa Joy is authentic, heart-centered, caring, and a very capable guide; she embodies the very principles that will lead you to discover this magnificence within yourself. Melissa has been teaching by my side for many years in numerous seminars throughout the world and is co-author of our best-selling second book, *The Physics of Miracles*. Knowing her has immeasurably enriched my life.

Here, once again, she brings her gentle wisdom and majestic influence to you through the written word. She will, in the pages of this marvelous book, take you to places in your personal journey that you may never have realized existed.

You are invited to go further into reality-creation than you may have imagined possible. Melissa has made stepping into this adventure simple by creating an entertaining virtual map for navigating the limitless playground of your infinite potential. Within this accomplished writing, she effortlessly decodes complex principles of hidden science and practical play that can unlock the door to your inner mastery. Throughout the holographically interwoven chapters, she explores the compelling yet sometimes perplexing fields of quantum physics and the new subtle energy physics, rendering them both interesting and understandable. Most importantly, she playfully reveals how they are relevant to your life by leading you gracefully through the field of the heart to experience your infinite potential.

Melissa Joy is so articulate, practical, and powerful in her approach to the intricacies of universal consciousness and the field of the heart that you can expect to be swept into a positively life-changing experience.

This book is an exquisite jewel of literature that is much more than just a book; it is an extraordinary event that can expand our consciousness and our ever-evolving beingness. Without a doubt, you are holding a timeless, unified expression of grace. Take this and read it. Drink it in. And may your heart be set afire with endless joy.

—Richard Bartlett, D.C., N.D., author of *Matrix Energetics* and *The Physics of Miracles*

Author's Note

Grace is the expression of the unconditional love that is universal consciousness. Grace is love, dancing with all possibilities equally. Grace is the spinning of the torsion fields that form matter, reality, and experience. Grace is consciousness experiencing itself in the moment as flow. Grace is available to all of us regardless of who we are, what we know, what we have experienced, or what we feel worthy of receiving. Grace is a freely available currency of potential that reconfigures us in every moment. Grace blankets us unconditionally, as a permeating thread woven into the fabric of love inherent in everything. Grace heals, transforms, transmutes, and transcends all circumstances. Grace is ever-present and abundantly available to us all. Grace is the calm unity in community. Grace is knowing without knowing how we know. Grace *is* love. Grace is the space where anything can happen. Grace is the cohesive, invisible container that unites morphic fields with the unified field of consciousness potential.

Grace is ever so playful, and everything we do, we can do from a state of play. We can approach interactive reality-creation as if it were a blank canvas awaiting our uniquely unlimited palette. Each of us is free to color inside or outside the lines, and even to create or transcend the lines if we so choose. As the ancient mystic Sri Aurobindo said, "There are no rules, there are only suggestions." Let us play as if there is no rules, only the suggestion that we all jettison our self-imposed, perceived limitations and access a state of potentiality through innocent childlike wonder. When we play in the field, the field plays through us. We become open doors that allow for infinite potential to express through us. We become portals for grace.

All of us are capable of becoming much more than we may previously have believed or thought possible. We already have what we desire within us. When we know and understand that we already are what we wish to become, we open ourselves to an unfolding reality where what is possible becomes probable, and what is probable becomes actual.

Come explore further this potential that is within you as together we plunge into the matrix of miracles and transformation. Let us uncover for ourselves that we are the magic in a sea of unlimited potential and that we can live that magic in a practical way in every moment of every day.

In-Joy,
Melissa Joy

Thank you.
In gratitude for All.

Introduction

Spirituality *is* practicality. Easier said than done—or is it?

Practicality often applies to the actual doing or being experience of something rather than to theories or ideas.

Too often, many of us separate our spiritual practice from our daily routines. However, to truly explore the limitless spiritual nature of our reality is to embrace the very fabric of consciousness that creates the totality of all experience. It is common to compartmentalize our exploration into consciousness as a spiritual journey that is separate from our everyday living. This distinction can defeat even the purpose of recognizing ourselves as spiritual beings who are having a human experience. To fully tap into consciousness potential, there is an implicit need to recognize the utility of an experience with practical ramifications in our daily living. In other words, we need to ask the important question, "How is this useful?"

We are indeed limitless beings, which means we are without end, limits, or boundaries. Yet, in the course of our life experiences, we sometimes forget our inherent ability to access the infinite potential that can be unveiled through expanding consciousness. Likewise, often we are confounded as to how to synthesize and integrate our awareness into practical application in our everyday lives.

It may seem as though many of us spend the majority of our lives struggling toward something or with someone. Actually, we are most often struggling with ourselves because we are unable to get out of our own way. We find ourselves stymied by our conditioning, our limiting beliefs, and our prior experiences. We may have resigned ourselves to the notion that life is something that happens to us. We often feel stuck. Our habitual ways of noticing and experiencing ourselves in a particular way often limits us from being able to notice or experience anything changing in our lives. We vacillate in fear of what may happen if we make the wrong choices. We actively participate in the *Parade of the Imagined Terribles*, anticipating all the ways our lives may go awry. We may see ourselves as victims of current or past circumstances or subject ourselves to those anxious anticipations of the dread that may come. In actuality, rarely do our experiences play out as our imagined worse case scenarios.

Reality might seem to happen to us, rather than noticing that we are powerful co-creators, partnering with universal consciousness to birth our varied experiences. In the desire to experience change or find more meaning in life, we often look outside ourselves for answers. We may seek a guru, a mentor, or a lover to teach us what we think we need to know to be more self-aware or different than we are. In doing so, we tend to allow our personal power to be siphoned off to somebody else or something else in hopes that we will be provided with answers. Often, we put that other person on a pedestal and then feel let down by perceived human frailty when they fall off. For various reasons, we are reticent to commit to becoming our own guru, our own mentor, or even our own lover. Ironically, we are the ones we have been waiting for. We must commit to ourselves first and foremost, and from there, everything can unfold from pure potentiality.

Life change does not need to be incessantly difficult. We are perhaps told that life is supposed to be full of challenges and contrast so that we can learn and grow. Yet, what we may find instead is that the sense of struggle creates more struggle. We struggle with our relationships, our careers, our friendships, our families, our finances, our day-to-day routines, and ourselves. Sometimes parts of our life appear to go smoothly while other components visibly unravel or stagnate. We may attempt to create safety by compartmentalizing our experiences.

"Why can't I change?" we ask ourselves. "What if I do change and still am not happy or satisfied? What is wrong with me?" Even if we think we know how to change, we may not recognize how to apply consciousness potential to transform our varied circumstances. We do not recognize that the way we do one thing is the way we do all things. We feel limited and fragmented and, as a result, we feel powerless.

Consider this: What if none of our limiting thoughts and beliefs is true? What if the real truth is that we are never powerless and always have options? What if everything we need to know to manifest our dreams is already available to us? What if there was a physics of transformation that consisted of heart-centered awareness, and to access it, all we had to do was to stop *not* accessing it?

Fortunately, through heart-centered awareness, we embrace wisdom by understanding that change is our natural state and that we have the power to allow it. Change flows from within us when we let go of the need for things to change—and when we let go of the need for things to remain the same. Our problems are not really problems at all, although we may currently perceive them as such. Rather, our problems are opportunities, options, and patterns of information. Perceived problems are placeholders in consciousness, seeking our attention. Placeholders are patterns of information that we have constructed to reflect back to us a piece of ourselves that we have yet to recognize inherently from within. Through awareness of our infinite potential and our natural ability to access different possibility states in any given moment, we can shift anything. Possibility states are transient unfoldings of our limitless potential prior to their actualization as experience, and they surround us in every moment. We are the solution to our problems. We have all the answers to our questions. We have within ourselves an inner strength and power. We do not need to limit that power or give it to others. It is our inherent birthright. We are universal consciousness experiencing itself. We are the technology of miracles. We are everything and, in that recognition, we have all the wisdom and potential we need to live extraordinary lives.

M-Joy Practically Speaking: Matrix Energetics and Living Your Infinite Potential is about learning to access your inherent infinite potential and apply it to everyday life. Gifts of awareness await your recognition within the pages of this book, whether you want to empower yourself, transform your relationships, heal a disease, move beyond a troubled past, change careers, earn more money, lose weight, or clean up the environment. Together, we will engage in an ongoing conversation with universal consciousness to create many useful transformative references and distinctions based on what is possible for all of us. Every one of us has the ability to experience a life of love, abundance, miracles, and wonder.

We will take a journey into the field of the heart to create a connection with universal consciousness, where we have direct access to our inner voice, our inner wisdom, and our inner chamber of unbounded potential. There are no limitations when accessing the field of the heart, and there are no limitations to the infinite methods of noticing, listening, and speaking from the field of the heart. We will come to understand that accessing the field of the heart provides us with a platform for experiencing instantaneous changes in our experience of reality. The physics and geometry of coherence support heart-centered awareness, and while it is not necessary to understand the science, this information propels us onto a trajectory for experiencing miracles, transformation, and unlimited possibilities in every facet of life. The technology of consciousness supported through heart-centered living is the science of the mystics and the ancient yogis. It is the science of torsion fields and miracles. This science is also the art and heart of Matrix Energetics (ME).

ME is a powerful field of consciousness potential that is accessible to everyone. Divinely inspired and originally created by Dr. Richard Bartlett in 2003, ME first began as a technique for healing, utilizing the now-famous Two Point for calibrating change. Dr. Bartlett's background as a chiropractor and naturopathic physician significantly influenced the original principles and form of the ME expression. As the technique took shape and increased in popularity, it evolved from a somewhat linear model for influencing health into a technology of consciousness, a field that interacts with all facets of reality and life.

The acclaimed Two Point has expanded to become a conversation with universal consciousness. It is a dance of awareness between what we are noticing now and what we have yet to notice that is different. This consciousness technology has grown into a powerful morphic field of information potential that is easily available and applicable to all who choose to interact with it. ME is much more than a technique. It is a way of being and interacting with an ever-expansive universe of unconditional love. From this state of being, anything is possible.

The system and field of ME is a universal language of consciousness potential that serves as a vehicle for personal and global transformation of physical, mental, emotional, social, spiritual, relational, financial, and self-referential patterns. Literally, it can be applied to anything anywhere and at any time. ME embodies the principles that consciousness is omnipresent and is within all that we encounter. As a vibrant, ever-expanding expression of grace and possibility, this morphic field is eager for you to explore the magical and amazing power abundantly available to you, and through you, as you choose to navigate through the realm of consciousness. This morphic field, which is based on what is possible and *not* on what is *not* possible, is a playground for miracles. It beckons you to play with and trust in it while inherently and continuously teaching you to play with and trust in yourself. Everyone—yes, everyone—can do this; the field of ME never discriminates and does not require any prior spiritual, medical, or educational training. The field graciously meets anyone and everyone precisely where they are on life's journey. It invites us all to go further and deeper into reality-creation than we may have previously imagined possible. Anything is possible, and the field of ME knows this, even if we have forgotten.

ME has been taught to tens of thousands of students around the world. In 2008, following several years of consciousness exploration and training with the founder Dr. Richard Bartlett, I joined him onstage as his co-teacher. We quickly discovered that an amazing synergy transpired each time we taught a seminar. Dr. Bartlett was quite adept at expanding students' awareness of consciousness and busting their reality boxes. He took them beyond their self-contained, limiting boundaries into the realm of the infinite. Once they had accessed that expanded state, I articulated an experiential under-standing of the field in a practical and relatively logical manner. We often entertained the question, How is this useful? In other words, how can you apply these meth-ods of exploring consciousness to life beyond this seminar? How can you apply this to your bank account, to your child's behavior, to your self-esteem, or to the traffic on your morning commute?

As the ME teachings evolved through Dr. Bartlett and me, students sometimes referred to me as Richard's translator. We laugh at this notion because we know that we simultaneously make both sense and nonsense. We are merely being our own unique expressions of this field that, together, we love so dearly. ME moves through us differently. When we teach ME, there is an expressed balance within the field of yin and yang, feminine and masculine, spiritual and scientific, esoteric and practical, expansive and foundational, abstract and linear. The field provides a synthesis of information that allows students to integrate their own polarities within themselves.

Amusingly, in many ways Dr. Bartlett is more linear and logical than he appears, and I am more intuitive and multidimensional than I may appear. Somewhere during the seminar experience, we invariably switch roles such that we are neither one way nor another exclusively. Rather, we are all of these aspects, as is everybody. We knowingly hold space for our students so that they may experience all aspects of the field and embody its inherent complexities and simplicities. It is this remarkable integration of the intuitive and the logical, the culmination of heart and mind, the synergy of the feminine and masculine, and the embrace of contrasting polarities that enables us all to transcend our perceived limitations and step into the totality of our essence as amazing beings.

My ongoing role in enhancing the teachings of ME has been to simplify the complex while embodying what is a possibility for all of us so that we can easily map multiple states from within. At times, I appear to represent the heart of the teachings, the unconditionally loving presence that mirrors our original divine blueprint. At other times, I seem to represent the logic that can pragmatically explain the science of miracles and transformation in an easy-to-understand fashion. And there are times when I am ridiculously silly. I am all of those facets, and yet none of them exclusively. We all are. We are all of those facets, and yet none of them exclusively. There is a time and a space for everything, and we invite ourselves and our students to embrace all aspects of beingness. Spirituality is practicality, and practicality is a flexibility of consciousness that is the epitome of ME.

Since my initial encounter with the field of ME in early 2006, my life has transformed dramatically in many extraordinary and practical ways. In some aspects, the changes have been so pronounced that I don't even recognize the person I used to be. Through the gifts reflected to us in the field of ME, I have shed parts of me that were more like masks and personas and I have found my integral being. I have re-remembered and become my true authentic self. I have learned to embody heart-centered awareness. I have transformed long-standing resistance to change, based on fear and doubt, into inner trust and allowing that nurtures my life to unfold as an expression of full potential. Whereas I previously felt paralyzed by indecision, I now genuinely know I am never stuck and that I always have choices. Grooves made by periodic past depression and unhappiness have been filled with joy, regardless of my external circumstances. Many former self-limiting ways of interacting with life have been significantly altered by virtue of having encountered ME. This powerful, amazing field of transformation has consistently mirrored back to me my own conscious potential and has provided me with limitless options for creating and recreating my life experiences.

With the unconditional support, love, and grace of the ME field, combined with personal surrender of self to this potential, we are free to choose transformation. We are the reason for the changes we experience, and the ME field supports this recognition every step of the way.

ME has taught me to trust in myself as an empowered, significant, unique expression of universal consciousness. It has taught me to let go of my attachments to limitations, which allows life situations to change. I have learned to consistently manifest desires into actual experiences.

Consistently, the field of ME has provided me with strategies for experiencing life differently—immediately. The ME field has helped to heal me of disease. The ME field has also helped me transform skewed self-perceptions and a sense of being separate from the all. In this recognition of the inherent connectivity of oneself to the all, there is a natural resonance created that enables us to access miracles.

This option is something ME offers to everyone, including you. The ME field does not discriminate or selectively choose who can benefit from its potential. Rather, with only a smidgen of curiosity, the ME field is accessible to every person who encounters it. Curiosity is key to unlocking the doors of our individual and collective potential. Curiosity is all it takes to open your awareness to the possibility that something in your life can indeed transform in the very next moment.

ME is a powerful springboard to personal evolution and higher consciousness. As a consciousness technology, the ME field functions via common denominators and core universal principles that, when accessed, allow an individual, community, and society to evolve, surrender into, manifest, and embody a higher consciousness. ME facilitates an ease of access to an expanded level of awareness that provides all of us with an equal opportunity to choose for ourselves to experience our boundless potential.

In many ways, this book goes beyond satisfying just a smidgen of curiosity; it will inspire your ability to access grace and unconditional love through the field of the heart, as they are the engine and the rocket fuel propelling ME.

This book, although it includes research, is mostly about search. Search is awareness expressing through our curiosity, synchronized with limitless potential. Join me as we search and discover the field of infinite possibilities.

ONE

Nature of Change

*Life is a series of natural and spontaneous changes. Don't
resist them—that only creates sorrow. Let reality be reality.
Let things flow naturally forward in whatever way they
like.*

—*Lao Tzu*

How can a book about transformation open an early
chapter with a quote that suggests that we "let reality be
reality?" I found myself questioning this as the chapter
began to unfold. However, in the same way I accepted
this quote as the perfect opener, it is also my acceptance
of what *is* that creates an allowance for, and an ability to,
change.

Go with the flow. The nature of change is flow.
Change occurs because it is an unobstructed current of
potential unfolding into experience. Any time we resist
the flow, we are resisting the stream that is carrying us
toward remembering who we really are—limitless
beings.

Most books on change and transformation provide
us with specific steps by which we can experience
ourselves differently. The assumption within most of
these instructions is that following the steps will make
us different or somehow better. We are expected to
digest suggestions from someone outside of ourselves.
These suggestions imply that something about us is not
right, or that we lack the right ingredients to live a more
expansive, joyful life.

A premise of this book is that everything is perfect.
There is nothing we need to do to be more than we
already are. We simply need to let go and enjoy the

journey. Some may not believe this yet, but inherent perfection does not require our belief in order to be. Beliefs can be limiting. We will discover that suspending beliefs is exactly what will assist our embodiment of this core truth.

Another premise upheld in this book is that consciousness is *everything,* and it persists regardless of what we think, believe, or disbelieve. It *is,* and we are direct extensions of, and connected to, everything. Therefore, you and I are everything in our completeness, already whole. This is not a book on oneness, per se; it is a book on uniqueness.

Uniqueness is expressed through our connection to unity. This is a book on embodying our True Authentic Self (TAS) as universal consciousness potential that is beyond what we have been told or have ever previously experienced. Each of us is a unique (uni-que) expression of universal (uni-versal) consciousness as it expands, creates, and experiences itself.

Let reality be reality: How is this statement useful in a book on consciousness potential, transformation, and change? Certainly, if we wanted reality to remain limited rather than unlimited, then we would not be interested in ME, the science and art of transformation, or a book about interactive reality-creation and co-creative change. However, letting reality be reality and embracing the concept of *letting go* is a fundamental component of the transformational process.

Truly, what is reality? We can never really know definitively what it is. We can only ever know reality through how we perceive it. Our lens of awareness provides us with a mechanism of noticing, perceiving, and experiencing that which we call reality.

By opening up our lens of awareness, we can receive and experience more of reality.

By modifying how we connect with reality—our vibration, also known as resonance—we can create a tapestry for a completely different experience.

Reality is fluid, like water. The more we learn to go with the flow, the more reality flows with us.

When resistance to *what is* metamorphoses into acceptance, there is a natural letting go of any negative charge that keeps the perspective of our reality locked into the polarity and duality of what we are attempting to discharge or transcend. In other words, a state of allowance and acceptance releases the unwanted charge against *anything*. A state of neutrality opens a portal for universal consciousness, as an expression of us, to notice itself as being *new-to-reality* (neutrality).

Neutrality is a portal-to-unity.

Neutrality allows for us to transcend the perceived limitations of duality by accepting duality as an extension of unity. Neutrality is the space-between-the-space of wanting something to change and noticing that it has not yet changed. Through awareness of unity and our connection to the all, we become active participants and co-creators with universal consciousness. We can easily leverage our personal awareness from a space where anything can unfold, where anything is possible.

Change

Change means to make or become different. To transform (trance-form) is to modify the form or expression of something. Our essence as limitless beings is a constant that does not change. Our experience or expression of that essence is the process of change, experienced through transformation.

Change is a constant. It does not happen because of us, but rather change happens in spite of us. The nature of change is that it happens. It happens with or without us. So, if we want to fully embrace it, we simply have to stop resisting it.

Change happens naturally when we are no longer resisting *what is,* and when we are no longer pushing against something or someone to create transformation.

Pushing against is a variation of resistance to flow. When we resist what is happening, we are actually holding information and experience in a separate, rigid construct of consciousness that empowers consciousness *not* to transform. When we cease to resist, that which has persisted begins to release its grip on us. What we hold on to holds on to us. When we let go of resistance, we return awareness to the all as pure potential, before it has separated out as experience. Let go into the all. Potential awaits our recognition to unfold in flow as experience.

That which we fight against or resist keeps us bound to its polarities and engaged in a perceived external war without, which creates a war within. When we are focused against something or someone, we are still resonating with it. It's a polarity conundrum.

An initial step toward changing the gauge of per- ceived experience is to release the resonance of being in opposition to anything. Let it be. Letting it be actually gives us leverage for things to change. When we are in a state of neutrality (new-to-our-reality), there is no charge on the positive or negative polarity. There is also no judgment. It just *is* in its entirety. Both sides of the polarity, positive and negative, are included. In the space between positive and negative is neutral, and that is where things will most readily change. Neutrality is all-inclusive. Inclusiveness is allowing, and allowance is the master currency of change.

Letting go or surrendering to the perceived need for things to change is different than giving up. Surrender- ing to *what seemingly is* provides for a letting go into *what seemingly is not.* There is no difference. Consciousness includes everything, and therefore, *what is not* is not distinct and separate from *what is.* They exist together.

They are the same. They are one. Giving up differs from letting go; when we give up, we are giving into *something* that appears to be what we do not want. We then continue to resonate with that *something,* with a sense of futility, so that what seems to lie beyond that *something* is excluded from awareness. Therefore, anything useful that is excluded from our awareness creates resistance to flow.

Letting go or surrendering is allowing, and allowing provides for a return to flow. When we allow for change, which is our natural essence, then change becomes an allowance for unlimited potential. Letting go is a liberation of attachments to *what is* and *what seemingly is not.* Letting go is an embrace of the all-inclusive, which is everything. Inclusion is freedom that has no opposite. It simply *is* and *is not,* together, as one. When everything is allowed, embraced, and included, there is no need to hang on to anything.

Amazingly, the universe knows the difference between truly letting go and pretending to let go. The former says, "I release this desire into the all and know it will be returned to me as manifestation and experience." Pretending sends the message, "I want this, and I know I am supposed to let go to allow it to unfold, but—just in case—I will hang on to this little part here while I pretend to trust." Fully letting go or surrendering triggers the physics of momentum and allows for the ripples of creation to reverberate in return.

Fully let go into the all and trust that your heartfelt desires will manifest as experience. Consider these words of Anaïs Nin: "Life is a process of becoming, a combination of states we have to go through. Where people fail is that they wish to elect a state and remain in it. This is a kind of death."

Freedom to Choose

From an all-inclusive space, we may then begin to make personal choices. Choice is our inherent ability to elect where we resonate in our awareness. Where we resonate creates our experience. So, while we may be allowing all of reality to be reality, it does not necessarily mean that we are experiencing everything. Until we allow for all to be included, we do not truly have a choice. We don't really have complete freedom or the ability to perceive or even discern our resonance if we are shackled by what we are clinging to, resisting, or pushing up against for *something* to transform.

Choose. Notice. Let go. Allow. Trust. Choose.

Practical Play

Choose. The universe is collaborating with us to be inspired by what we desire. The desires that well up from the field of the heart are powerful indicators or maps to help us choose wisely. Our choices are always extensions of universal consciousness. From the all-inclusive vantage of universal consciousness, choices are neither inherently positive nor inherently negative. Just choose.

Notice. Notice what is different, not what is the same.

Why does it seem so difficult for us to experience change? Perhaps the key here is the word *seem,* since our perceptions and attachments to experiences *not* changing are what keep us tethered to more of the same. Too often, we notice what is the same, and not what is different. When we notice what is different, we begin to perceive change as it is unfolding. Where we resonate, so we experience.

Noticing what is different moves awareness into resonance with the change that is *already* happening. We have a tendency to continually notice what is *not* chang-

16

ing, which usually reinforces the idea that things are the same. If all we notice is that *something* is not changing, then that *something* is all we are capable of noticing and subsequently experiencing. However, accepting *what is* and then noticing what is *different* within the all-inclusive is-ness establishes a connection between *what is* and *what is different,* so that *what is* becomes the change we want to experience.

Let go. Desiring and focusing on the need to let go keeps us in resistance to letting go. Let go of the need to let go. The more we try to let go, the more we hang on to what we wish to release. When we let go, we are no longer creating a separation between who we are and what we desire to experience. We also are no longer paying attention to the perceived gap between who we are and what we desire to experience.

We may feel frustrated when we are in the gap between what we desire in our hearts and its outward manifestation. What we may not recognize is that simply perceiving ourselves as being stuck in the gap between two experiences is, in fact, progress and movement. Perceiving this is a marker for our awareness; it declares that we are never stifled because we are in perpetual motion and are continuously learning and evolving en route. Let go into the gap and notice that the gap is no longer there. When we let go into the gap, we create a bridge from our heart's desire to its manifestation, and then we *notice what we notice* as we traverse the bridge.

Letting go lets in *all* that we actually are, which is universal consciousness and pure potentiality. From this powerful space we can then choose where to resonate so that desired experiences will flow through us. Let go.

Allow. Letting go of letting go quite naturally leads us to accept what is showing up in life and perceive it as a pattern or placeholder in awareness that does not limit or define us. Allow whatever is showing up to exist without resisting it. Simply notice whether the pattern is changing or not changing without any judgment or attachment. Noticing what you notice is the art of getting into a neutral state, or of being in a state of neutrality.

Trust. Trust can simply be a matter of awareness. Trust where your attention goes when you ask what it would be like if you could accept what you want to change without resistance. What does it feel like? From this state of neutrality and allowing, ask if the pattern or experience could express in a different way? Do not define how or when or why. Simply ask and allow the answer to emerge. Trust what surfaces.

Trust establishes a coherent connection between our True Authentic Self (TAS) and our consciousness potential. The connection between TAS and consciousness potential is an unbroken connection that does not require faith or certainty. Trust is awareness of connection.

Choose, notice, let go, allow, trust, and choose. When this happens, everything flows coherently. When we stop resisting the flow, it's like letting go of the oars of the canoe that we are laboring to paddle upstream and instead allowing ourselves to float effortlessly downstream with the current. Feel the giddiness of the experience and holler, "Wheeee!" with great joy.

Change is flow, and both are as natural as breathing. Similarly, as a figure of speech, we can say that we breathe in consciousness potential and we exhale experience. Noticing, letting go, and allowing reality to be reality from a state of neutrality is key to experiencing change. Consider that letting go leads to allowing, and that trusting in that process creates coherence with universal consciousness.

Heart-centered awareness, which I will cover more extensively later in this book, naturally enables our awareness to transcend the perceived limitations of duality, polarity, and contrast. There is nothing to do, and no-thing to compare. Heart-centered awareness taps into a well of limitless information and energetic potential. It embodies the space of all-inclusion and personal power, because there is a knowingness that transpires such that there is nothing to exert power over. Remember, no-thing is separate from that which is itself—which is you, which is every-one, which is every-thing, which is nothing simultaneously. Heart-centered awareness allows us to access the nature of our limitless self and allows for change to flow as a natural progression of the expression of universal consciousness.

We are universal consciousness, and through us, limitless potential experiences itself as form and matter. Information unfolds as *inform-in-action,* creating our experiences. We are containers into which universal consciousness, as limitless potential, pours itself to be actualized. Universal consciousness is contained within us *as us* and is limited only by our limited perception. As a container of consciousness, the more flexible we can be, the more that universal consciousness can pour forth *as us.* We have the inherent ability to embody a flexibility of consciousness, through transcending what is conditioned unconditionally for change.

TWO

Universal Consciousness and Unlimited Potentials

Consciousness is a word worn smooth by a million tongues. Depending upon the figure of speech chosen it is a state of being, a substance, a process, a place, an epiphenomenon, an emergent aspect of matter, or the only true reality.
— *George Miller*

What is universal consciousness? Well, before we attempt to define it, we must acknowledge that any description of universal consciousness is merely a description of it, and is not actually it. As it is with defining a banana, we understand that the description is not an actual banana. The description is only a signpost pointing to the banana. Defining universal consciousness, like describing a banana, provides only an interpretation of how we perceive, feel, or know it through our personal experience. Similarly, an attempt to describe the science of *banana* or of *universal consciousness,* or the structural elements that give them both form and substance, still would not be *banana* or *universal consciousness.* Universal consciousness is the wisdom above and beyond the banana, the banana itself, and everything that is experienced *in relation to* the banana. Universal consciousness is also everything else that exists, has ever existed, and may ever exist.

Universal consciousness is the mechanism for everything and *is*—everything.

The essence of universal consciousness has been described as spirit, light, love, nature, torsion, and ether. It has also been described as us. In other words, we are universal consciousness. We don't experience universal consciousness, rather, universal consciousness *is*, and it experiences itself through us.

Our individual perception of that which is universal consciousness can be a prism or a prison, depending upon our flexibility or resistance to flow.

So, what is universal consciousness, really? Perhaps it isn't what we think it is. In fact, it may even exist apart from our thinking. *Merriam-Webster* defines consciousness as "the quality or state of being aware, especially of something within oneself. The state or fact of being conscious of an external object, state, or fact." Therefore, that which is conscious has perspective when observing what it perceives.

However, the consciousness I am referring to, universal consciousness, is impersonal in nature and spans far beyond individual awareness, space-time, and beyond anything we may think we know definitively. I am referring to universal consciousness as the all. In its entirety, it is void of perspective and identity because it includes all vantage points as part of itself. Anything we say consciousness is will merely be a description or a signpost for what it actually is. Defining an individual's perspective of consciousness does not define consciousness, either. It only describes *a perspective* of consciousness. In this book I am utilizing particular language and definitions for consciousness in an attempt to invite everyone to the same page. Nonetheless, this does not mean that everyone must have the same perspective about something with an inherent nature that is undifferentiated and limitless. Any and all definitions serve as a single point of reference called *perspective,* even if that perspective proclaims that there are infinite points of pointlessness to what is being defined.

It is not important that we are all on the same page with respect to consciousness, or to any perspective offered here. Truth is ultimately a deeply personal experience, and this book is not about consensual truth.

This book is about understanding your own truth for yourself regarding the nature of your own reality as a limitless being. In this book, we will journey together to explore consciousness, the nature of reality, and living our infinite potential.

If something within these writings provokes a charge or sparks your interest, then by all means, pay attention! That is a clue or signpost to your awareness, telling you that you may have accessed resistance, rigidity, potentiality, possibility, opportunity, or awesomeness.

We want to continuously challenge our notions about reality, particularly those that are limiting in nature, so that we can consciously and interactively re-create the experience of ourselves as limitless beings.

As defined in this book, universal consciousness includes everything and excludes nothing. It is my experience that everything comes from universal consciousness.

Whether we are esoteric, scientific, united, or divided about what universal consciousness actually is, our approach to defining it appears to make little difference to universal consciousness itself. That which is everything and is impersonal in nature does not seem to care what we call it or how we describe it. Consciousness itself does not come across as judgmental or discriminatory about beliefs, perspectives, opinions, or concepts—even if we sometimes are. As discussed in this book, universal consciousness includes everything. Everything is universal consciousness experiencing itself. Therefore, universal consciousness *is*. . . . We are . . . I am . . . and you are All That Is. Om Tat Sat.

Consciousness Illuminates

Healing is to be in the light of our own consciousness. Healing is an inner light, which exists as a natural radiance around a person. This inner light is in itself a healing force beyond words. This inner light disperses darkness,

like when you light a candle in a dark room and the dark-
ness disappears by itself. This inner light exudes a subtle
influence through its mere presence. The more the light in
our own consciousness is lit, the more it creates a subtle ef-
fect in the world.
—*Swami Dhyan Giten,* Presence—Working from Within

Many references throughout many spiritual traditions draw parallels between consciousness and light. Even our bodies appear to be composed of light. Physicists have noted that our bodies are made of biophotons, and biophotons are light. It has been scientifically proven that every cell in the body emits more than 100,000 light impulses, or photons, per second. These light emissions, found in all living things, are called biophotons and have been found to be the driving mechanism behind all biochemical reactions.[1]

The Russian embryologist Alexander Gurwitsch did initial research establishing the role of light in living processes. In 1923, Gurwitsch established a strong hypothesis that every living cell emits light. In the 1970s, the work of German scientist Fritz Popp expanded further upon biophoton theory, providing ample experimental evidence. Fritz Popp discovered that DNA both emits and absorbs biophotons and that the health of living creatures could be determined by the subtle energy of the biophotons they emit.

Light, Information, and Torsion in the Synchronized Universe

According to MIT- and Princeton-educated physicist Dr. Claude Swanson in his Synchronized Universe model:

> the new sciences of biophotons and torsion fields provide a bridge between two views of life: the old twentieth century view of an organism as a chemical machine and the emerging view of life as communication and energetic flows.[2]

Dr. Swanson goes on to state:

> Bio-photons (light) create the three-dimensional hologram, which controls growth and healing. It creates and interacts with torsion fields which extend beyond the body, and create the aura. . . . The ability of intention and visualization to alter DNA transcription, changing cell biology, is one of the modern breakthroughs which help us understand the close connection between consciousness and biophotons.[3]

Dr. Swanson further maintains that

> with the creation of each biophoton, there is also a torsion wave. Torsion is a widespread and important form of radiation, which couples particle spins together, and propagates through space as a twisting wave in the metric. It results in a variety of new phenomena. These effects have been studied extensively for the past forty years, at multiple research centers in Russia. Their most important conclusion is that this torsion force is exactly the same as subtle energy.[4]

Simply stated, the body is made of light, also known as biophotons. Biophotons create a hologram informing the body to grow and heal. This hologram of light creates torsion fields (spin) and also transmits and receives information from resonant torsion fields (spin) around the body.

Furthermore, extensive Russian research has shown that torsion fields, presumed to be everywhere in the fabric of the universe, are able to transmit and receive information. What is more, the communication between torsion fields is not limited by time and space.

In other words, torsion fields can transmit and receive information, including thoughts, instantly from anywhere to anywhere. Biophotons are considered the "intermediating link between local/linear and non-local/non-linear field effects."[5]

Torsion fields appear to be a form of subtle energy that is present everywhere. As you will learn later in this book, torsion fields may be containers for information as inform-in-action, creating geometries for form, matter, and experience.

Light as a Source of Life

Light as a source of life may be that which is the essence of universal consciousness. Remarkably, according to Terrence McKenna, photons of light apparently have no antiparticles.[6]

Does this imply that there is no dualism in the world of light? If there is no opposite to light, which is our essence, then darkness may not be darkness at all, but merely light distanced from itself. If we are made of light, and light has no opposite, then our fundamental essence of light might be all there is. Thus, our perceived experience of duality may not be a split or polarization of light and dark at all, but instead a degree of how far our awareness can distance itself from the light that we are.

Consciousness Creates

If universal consciousness were to have a desire or a purpose, then perhaps it would be to create. Universal consciousness appears to create as a way of becoming more aware of itself. In the same way that we each have personal perspective, universal consciousness appears to create to experience itself through various perspectives, expressions, reflections, and distinctions. It occurs to me that consciousness *sees* itself in all its creations and is not separate from them.

If this is true, then all distinctions extend from, and are still connected to, universal consciousness, which includes all of us. The individual expressions that universal consciousness makes through us become our *sole* (soul) signature. It is what makes us unique. Individual (in-divide-u-all) and individuality (in-divine-duality) refer to our unique experience of ourselves, not as separate and apart from universal consciousness but as direct extensions of it.

What Is Consciousness Potential?

As referenced in this book, universal consciousness creates from unlimited potential. Consciousness potential is *no-thing*. It can be described as *nothing* because it has not yet expressed itself as *something*. Consciousness potential is universal consciousness *before* consciousness creates, actualizes, and/or experiences. Consciousness potential is void of distinctions or boundaries, and therefore, it also has no limitations. Undifferentiated consciousness potential is limitless, formless, weightless, timeless, spaceless, thoughtless, and totally free.

Referring to the all as *no-thing,* as consciousness potential, actually facilitates access to it. All we need to do is become aware of consciousness potential. But how do we become aware of something that has nothing to be aware of? We begin by letting go of our sense of being separate. Awareness from an expanded perspective, that is inclusive of everything as consciousness, and *no-thing* as consciousness potential, allows for that potential to express itself more readily through us.

Consciousness potential is also that which is unconditional love. Unconditional love is the cohesive force that unifies *all,* a thread that weaves through the fabric of the universe. It is not "I love you." It is Love IS. Unconditional love is not love as we humans have become accustomed to it, with all its parameters, expectations, and limitations. Consciousness potential as unconditional love is impersonal in nature. It is love void of all conditions.

Consciousness potential is *love is* as a preconditioned essence; it is love that exists regardless of human relations, emotions, perceptions, or forms.

As a concept, love is often misunderstood, and therein lies the potential difficulty in accepting that unconditional love is everything and *no-thing.* Our limited concepts of love have been personified and deeply distorted into conditioned states. The love that creates all, heals all, and transforms all is actually deeply impersonal and without conditions.

Certainly some expressions of love are carrier waves for transformation and healing, but those expressions are not what truly heal. Those expressions reconnect us to the stateless potential of condition-less love. They reflect back to us our natural essence as consciousness potential. It is not that human love heals, per se, but that love itself reflects back to us the wholeness that is inherently within each and every one of us.

Expressions of unconditional love, no longer uncon-ditioned by virtue of being conditioned into an expres-sion, are powerful, coherent placeholders for our potential return to wholeness and connection with source as universal consciousness. Compassion, empa-thy, laughter, and friendship, expressed as supportive gestures, a kind word, or a gentle caress are just a few of many mirrored reflections that serve to nurture our consciousness potential back into flow, as well-being. Unconditional love as consciousness potential is what we are in our true essence. Therefore, an expression of love from another or from oneself is like receiving a homeopathic remedy for awareness. We remember, we resonate with, we receive, we allow, and we return to our natural state of wholeness, which is then inherently reflected as wellness.

Wellness, or well-being, is a natural flow that is ex-pressed through a body of information (in-form-in-action) that serves as a vehicle for universal conscious-ness. Thus, wellness is a conditioned expression of consciousness, of love, flowing through form from its original condition-less state. Ultimately, well-being is consciousness potential expressing itself as love and light through us.

Although we may be experiencing conditions that seem far removed from our true essence of love expressed as light, we are much more than our conditions. We are much more than our problems. We are much more than anything we are choosing or not choosing to experience in any moment or over time. We are universal consciousness and unlimited potential. Though we may have moved our awareness away from noticing this as part of our experiences, we always have the inherent ability to return to this knowingness. With this recognition, we can recondition our experiences and limitlessly create new experiences. We can tap into our consciousness potential and open up to knowing and recognizing ourselves as more than what we have previously experienced.

Synchronicity

If you were to experience yourself as more than your personal experiences, your beliefs, your thoughts, and your conditioning—*and* if you were to notice that you are connected to consciousness potential—what might you notice? If you knew how this expansion in awareness might change your experience of yourself and the experiences of others, what might you notice?

What occurs to me when I ask this question is an awareness of synchronicity in everything. The phenomena of synchronicity was conceptualized and coined by Swiss psychologist Carl Gustav Jung in the 1920s. He used the term *synchronicity* to describe the experience of two or more seemingly unrelated events being observed as happening together in a meaningful manner.[7]

"Synchronicity," said Jung, "is the coming together of inner and outer events in a way that cannot be explained by cause and effect and that is meaningful to the observer."[8] In other words, awareness of synchronicity means noticing the interconnected patterns of everything and recognizing that there is no such thing as coincidence. Although we may be the meaning-makers of our experiences, taking note of synchronicities when they occur can facilitate greater awareness of our connection to universal consciousness and unlimited potentials.

Synchronicity can show up for us in myriad ways.

A common way that we become aware of synchronicity is by noticing numbers on a timepiece. For example, you might notice that each time you look at a clock, watch, or digital device, it reads: 1:11, 2:22, 3:33, 11:11, or 12:12. No matter what leads you to check the time, when you actually look at it, the reading consistently reflects a unity and a connectedness.

Events are another way we can notice synchronicity. For instance, you may find that you are thinking about buying a new set of socket wrenches, and the next day, without knowing this, your neighbor gifts you a set for having mowed his lawn while he was on vacation. Or maybe, en route to the grocery store, you are contemplating calling a friend with whom you haven't spoken in a year. Synchronistically, as you are getting out of your car, you look up and see your friend standing in the entryway of the store.

Synchronicity may also show up as everything effortlessly falling into place. The resources needed to make something happen are available to us, as though they were perfectly timed to present in the exact moment the need was realized. Or maybe the resources necessary for a special event become available in a unique or unexpected way, soon after you recognize the desire and the need. For example, you consider taking a consciousness technology seminar but you're not sure you'll have the funds to attend. You commit to going anyway, despite not having the adequate resources, and lo' and behold, the next day you receive an unexpected tax refund for the exact amount of the tuition. This is perfect timing. Perfect timing is an aspect of synchronicity.

Synchronicity often shows up through music. Sometimes, a song will come to mind that I have not heard in many years. I might be humming its tune and turn on the radio only to notice that the very same song is playing. This is always a clue for me to pay attention.

If this kind of music synchronicity occurs for you, listen closely to the lyrics. What are they saying? Who is the band? What information comes to mind when you connect to the total experience of the music?

Sometimes the message of synchronicity is not literal, but is instead figurative, because synchronicity shows up through symbolic representations of information. Symbolism occurs as a patterned language of universal consciousness.

While preparing the framework for an upcoming seminar, I had this kind of resonance synchronicity happen to me. I kept hearing a song in my mind that I have not listened to in several years. *Apparently* out of nowhere, the song kept repeating in my awareness, over and over again. Not surprisingly, when I turned on the radio, the song was playing there, too. Noting the synchronicity, I reviewed the lyrics and initially concluded the message it contained was about releasing a pattern with my family. So, feeling grateful, I released the pattern through forgiveness and let it go.

Interestingly, over the next several weeks, I kept hearing that same song both in my mind and on the radio. I considered that perhaps I was being prompted to play the song at my upcoming seminar.

Soon thereafter, I better understood the meaning of the synchronicity. While continuing to frame the seminar, which was flowing rather nicely, I sensed that a pivotal piece of the project was still missing. Again, the dated song came to mind. Aha! I finally made the *bigger* literal and figurative connection. The name of the song

31

was also the surname of a person who had written something that quite obviously was the missing piece of my project. I had reviewed the information the prior day and was sitting on the fence about including it. Now I had my answer. Yes. It was a huge Aha! and ha-ha moment. I consider the recognition of synchronistic connections ab-soul-utely, duh-lighful!

It is interesting to consider that we are often able to notice synchronicities in retrospect. We look back at the so-called random events of our lives and are able to easily recognize how circumstances were interconnected and interwoven. We notice that even the events we perceived as negative were part of the bigger tapestry of our experiences. We may see the inherent perfection of all of the choices and circumstances that led us to become exactly who we are right now. We may see the synchronicity of our lives and finally realize that we are part of a greater whole. Synchronicity is always available to us. As a gift to yourself, open up your awareness and let synchronicity in.

Jung astutely noted that synchronicity is more likely to occur when we are in a state of heightened awareness.[9] In other words, when we are excited about the synchronistic events, they tend to occur more frequently. So, allow yourself to be delighted and surprised by the unfolding of events that are invariably connected. When you do so, synchronicity can return you to a state of flow. Synchronicity can remind you that all circumstances are patterned connections, and that everything is working together in harmony. You can go with the flow. When we pay attention to synchronicity, we naturally gain a deeper understanding of our true authentic self with universal consciousness and unlimited potential.

Practical Play with Universal Consciousness and Unlimited Potential

- Think of a recent event or experience that seemed synchronistic to you. How did it make you feel?
- What elements of the experience can you invite into your awareness, now?
- Do you feel excitement, wonder, delight, or amazement?
- In what ways can you carry these heightened sensations with you so that you increase the likelihood of noticing more synchronicity in your life?

Universal consciousness and its unlimited potential is what we are. We always have a direct line to this connection because it is never broken. Simply notice. While sometimes we may feel as though we are alone on our journey, we are all-one with that which *is* everything. Consider that there is a divine plan interwoven throughout the threads and fabric of universal consciousness that can be fully expressed through the field of the heart and through grace. That divine plan is to unite us with the full recognition of who we truly are as limitless beings.

That plan is to remember. All we need to do to access what is available is to ask, open, trust, receive, allow, and choose.

THREE

Reality and Experience
Morphic Fields and Memes

If the doors of perception were cleansed every thing would appear to man as it is, Infinite.
—William Blake, The Marriage of Heaven and Hell

Reality is virtually a symbolic representation of patterns of information. Notice the patterns and come explore the connections with the interlocking grids of consciousness that permeate the all that is.

As beings of limitless potential, we actually can choose where to resonate, which helps to shape our experiences. Resonate with fields of limitations, and limitations are what you will encounter within yourself and everything around you. Resonate with fields of limitless potential, and anything is possible. Through consciousness potential and resonance, we can expand our apertures of awareness to experience the full expression of ourselves as limitless beings. Through awareness, we can become more adept at recognizing the informational fields with which we are connecting that influence our experiences. What we take resonance with, takes residence within us.

Consider that experience is a function of light, information, and resonance. As previously stated, we are beings of light. In my experience, that which is light interacts with information as potential through morphic fields of consciousness.

These interactions create connections or resonances with the information contained in morphic fields. What unfolds from the information within morphic fields of consciousness is, in turn, expressed through all of us as energy and experience.

We can gain indepth understanding of the science of morphic field resonance by referring to the extensive pioneering work of biologist Rupert Sheldrake, Ph.D. His groundbreaking scientific theory on morphic fields has transformed how we understand consciousness, biology, and behavior. Practically speaking, morphic field resonance may also further explain the nature of change and transformation.

According to Dr. Sheldrake:

> The word morphic field comes from the Greek *morphe,* meaning form. Morphic fields organize the form, structure and patterned interactions of systems under their influence. . . .
>
> All self-organizing systems are wholes made up of parts, which are in turn lower-level wholes themselves— such as organelles in cells, cells in tissues, tissues in organs, organs in organisms, organisms in social groups. At each level, the morphic field gives each whole its characteristic properties, and coordinates the constituent parts.
>
> The fields responsible for the development and maintenance of bodily form in plants and animals are called morphogenetic fields. In animals, the organization of behavior and mental activity depends on behavioral and mental fields. The organization of societies and cultures depends on social and cultural fields. All these kinds of organizing fields are morphic fields.[1]

Consider that the experience of your personal reality will vary immensely depending upon your resonance with social, cultural, psychological, and even biological morphic fields. Social morphic fields overlap with cultural morphic fields that can, in turn, influence psychological and biological morphic fields, and vice versa.[2]

According to Dr. Sheldrake, a morphic field is "a field within and around a morphic unit." In turn, a morphic field organizes a morphic unit's characteristic structure and pattern of activity. He continues:

> Morphic fields underlie the form and behavior of holons or morphic units at all levels of complexity. The term morphic field includes morphogenetic, behavioral, social, cultural, and mental fields. Morphic fields are shaped and stabilized by morphic resonance from previous similar morphic units, which were under the influence of fields of the same kind.[3]

Morphic Fields of Habit

> *Through repetition, the patterns morphic fields organize become increasingly probable, increasingly habitual. The force that these fields exert is the force of habit.*
> *—Rupert Sheldrake, Ph.D.*

"The force that these (morphic) fields exert," states Sheldrake, "is the force of habit."[4] Hmmm? And we know that habits can be broken, changed, or transformed through awareness. And we know that new habits can be formed with finesse and focused intent.

Practically speaking, morphic fields serve as containers for consciousness; they hold patterned information that gives shape to our experiences. If morphic fields develop and evolve through similarity, repetition, and resonance, then consider that we can change our resonance with morphic fields in the same way that we change our habits. We can choose a different focus and change the programmed behavior. Through our intention and attention, without tension, we can affect our resonance with these fields of information that affect our experience.

Habituated Consciousness In-Forms Us

Consider the global morphic field of *fear*. In many aspects this field of fear is based on the fear of death. Not surprisingly, most fears actually stem from a core fear of death, which is a morphic field unto itself. With a bit of awareness, it is easy to observe that the morphic fields of *religion* and *politics* have been reinforced and perpetuated with and through the fear of death field.

The global morphic field of *fear* may have started long, long ago with a holon or a morphic unit of thought. Perhaps fear was simply an inherent, perceived threat to survival. After all, a hungry saber-toothed tiger used to be a realistic threat to survival. When challenged by a tiger, the fear of death resonated, as did the primal instinct to either run from or slay the tiger. In this sense, the fear was valid and a perceived matter of survival, not only of self, but of others, as well. When we perceive a threat to life, our autonomic nervous system takes over. We are super-revved with adrenaline and super-charged with a chemical rush of energy that enables us to respond with amazing speed, clarity, and precision.

When challenged by the presence of a tiger, imagine for a moment that our ancestors chose to run from the beast and, thankfully, survived. The gallant survivors would have shared with their tribal community the idea of this very real threat, which was based on a very real experience, and wisely advised everyone of the optimal known survival options, which were to either run from tigers or slay tigers.

Imagine that, as time went on, other tribal members encountered tigers while going about their daily rituals. Sensing fear, supercharged with adrenaline, and re-calling the two optimal *known* survival options previous-ly shared with the community, the threatened men chose to kill the tiger. Heroically, they returned to the village and glorified their hunting stories by inserting bits of creative and exaggerated details to impress the ladies.

Fear was now being further propagated throughout the community in conversational gossip regarding anything that might threaten survival. In addition, those individuals who had encountered a tiger decided to appoint themselves to encode and create rules for the rest of the tribe to keep everyone safe. With their newly self-appointed leadership roles intact, the great leaders again sensed, physiologically and energetically, a pumping and surging of adrenaline. Morphic units, as thoughts and feelings of power, were embedded into the growing morphic field of *fear*. It is easy to see how the morphic field of *power structure* was birthed and enabled to protect the community by exploiting the community's vulnerabilities and fears. This power structure, in turn, created yet another morphic field, *perceived safety*.

As communal members ourselves, we are sometimes grateful for the programmed rules that encode for optimal and evolving options. As our options have evolved, we not only can *run from* tigers and *slay* tigers, but now we also can *hide from* tigers. We can also listen to our fearless newly appointed leaders and entrust our survival to the chosen ones who know because they have both encountered and survived a threat referred to as *tigers*.

It was not abnormal and is not abnormal for tribal members to become increasingly fearful given the limited available choices for tiger-survival. Through such debilitating fear, people become entirely dependent upon the directives of community leaders. This is how relinquishing the personal power of choice to our leaders evolves. This is often why we, as tribal members, succumb and do exactly as we are told.

This is an example of how the morphic resonance of fear increases, perpetuates, and evolves. Fear is literally in the air. In response to the fear of death, the fear of surviving, and/or the fear of fear itself, women and children in many cultures are no longer able to roam freely because they are *perceived* to be more vulnerable than men. Accordingly, women often habitually rely upon men to protect them and their children from the *tigers*. Children grow up fearing the *tigers* or *perceived threats,* and may even train their whole lives to fight against the *tigers* or *perceived threats.*

Literally and metaphorically, the real threat is not the tigers, but the village on the other side of the mountain. It could be that the adjacent village's tee-pees are getting too close to *our river,* which is *our tribe's* main source of water. People perceive this territorial movement as a threat and automatically associate it with the *tiger.* Leaders encourage this fear-based perception. Communal resonance with the deeply engrained habit to *run from* the tiger or to *kill* the tiger kicks in. *Hiding* is not an option because communal resources are threatened. Unwilling to uproot an entire village in search of new land, tribal members choose the perceived optimal option in response to the *perceived* fear. The option chosen is to *kill* the tiger, except this time the killing is a war that decimates the opponent's entire community. *We* conquer the tigers or the perceived threats rather than the fear itself. *We* have now added additional morphic units of *survival* to the morphic field of *fear.* The idea, or morphic unit, of *war* is thus born, which eventually becomes a global morphic field unto itself, as well.

Instead of choosing to share the flow of the river and the endless supply of water that nature has always provided, we habitually choose to respond with fear. Instead of choosing to communicate and collaborate with each other, we unfortunately choose to compete with and destroy each other.

Fast-forward to modern times where the actual threat of the tiger is no longer imminent or even valid. *Fear of survival* has taken on a much bigger placeholder in the global morphic field of fear. Fear permeates everything. We no longer even know what it is we are really afraid of because so many confusing messages and perceived threats saturate society. Fear has become something we relate to as separate from ourselves. We perceive fear as coming from a force out there, outside of ourselves, rather than something coming from within us. We do not see fear as a part of our own resonance. Interestingly enough, we have never even met the *tiger*, and we often do not realize that the *tiger* is within us.

As we can see, morphic fields of *religions* and *governments* have formed, evolved, and been perpetuated from the global morphic field of *fear*. In turn, these resonant fields have made contributions to the ever-expanding growth of the global morphic field of fear. The feedback and reinforcement are synergistic.

Religious and political morphic fields promise honesty to, protection of, and ever-lasting life to the people. There is nothing ultimately wrong with religion or politics per se, except that these morphic fields are often fertile breeding grounds for fear. Most of our wars are fought in the name of religion and politics. Ironically, wars perpetuate the very fear of survival and fear of death we seek to avoid.

Societies have been programmed for fear. The morphic field of fear is all around us. Media feeds this field by regurgitating news draped in terror. "Be afraid!" is the message. "Terrible things are happening everywhere!" News is slanted and tainted to ensure that our focus is fear-based. There are a few good-news networks on the Internet, but not everyone has access to them. Mainstream news networks know that fear grosses higher ratings and that higher ratings, in turn, feed the global morphic field of *economy*. In many ways, we have been programmed for fear and naively tune into news as a matter of habit. News is not new news. It has become a morphic field of *habit*.

Even conspiracy theories, while attempting to reveal the truth of certain power-elite structures that also thrive on fear, are fear-propagating memes. Any conspiracy theory that puts us in resonance with something that is supposedly conspiring-against us is no better than the so-called truth the theory seeks to reveal.

There is a big difference between sharing information as an offering so that people can make informed choices for themselves about what to believe and spreading supposed truths that are cloaked in fear. The former, sharing information, allows for choices of resonant truth. The latter, spreading supposed truths cloaked in fear, perpetrates separative fear. All fear is a deception of perception.

Universal consciousness with its infinite potentials does not conspire against us through divisive perspectives of limiting fears. Universal consciousness inspires to create more of itself *with* us as unified and expansive love.

The morphic field of fear keeps us bound in limitations. When we are resonating in fear, we tend to give away our personal power. When we are resonating in fear, we tend to forget we have options. When we are resonating in fear, we often forget who we are. When we are resonating in fear, we forget we are love. When we are resonating in fear, we are unable to share love.

What if fear is simply love in a confused, or confused (conceptually fused), state? What if fear, like darkness that is light distanced from itself, is simply a distancing of love from itself? What if fear is just love con-formed and con-firmed by distorted associations that prevent it from recognizing itself? What if fear is simply a movement in awareness away from the love that we are?

Consider fear of death. Perhaps fear of death is instead love of life. Consider fear of rejection. Perhaps fear of rejection is instead love for others. Consider fear of failure. Perhaps fear of failure is instead just love of personal growth and accomplishment. It appears that all fears are instead forms of love turned inside-out and upside-down. Various distortions of love that are masked in fear can take on corresponding resonant expressions that bear no resemblance to our perceptions and/or understandings of love. Murder. Rape. War. Tyranny. But at the root of these distorted fears, and corresponding, contorted morphic fields, there is always a love of something deeper.

When we begin to recognize our personal resonance with morphic fields of limitation, such as fear, we can dismantle our personal connection to these fields and individually tune into more expansive fields. We can do so by recognizing the programs, or memes, that are keeping us contained by or resonating with specific morphic fields.

When we unplug from morphic fields of limitations, such as fear, it is akin to taking back our personal and our collective power. It is akin to neutralizing the morphic units we may have unknowingly contributed to, morphic units that provide a charge that affords more power, shape, and form to a given field. This charge, in turn, generates a more fearful resonance, thus creating more personal, fear-based experiences. Thankfully, we can take back these charges with no further accumulated interest.

When we choose to re-appropriate our personal morphic units of limitation to morphic fields of expansion, we ultimately experience more for ourselves. In turn, the morphic fields of expansion we resonate with grow along with us.

Morphic fields are all around us. When we become more aware of them, we can learn to modify our resonance and therefore change our experience so we can live more expansive lives. We can intentionally tap into specific morphic fields of potential to assist us in our experiential journey of limitless living.

Memes, Seems, and Program Machines

Memetics is another emerging scientific paradigm that provides insight on how much of our behavior, instead of being individually driven, is the product of viral thought replication. Memetics is a theoretical and empirical science that studies the replication, spread, and evolution of memes.[5]

A meme is an information pattern in an individual's memory that can be copied to another individual's memory.[6]

The study of memes began with evolutionary biologist Richard Dawkins. His pioneering work is detailed in his 1976 book, *The Selfish Gene*.

According to Dr. Dawkins:

> Examples of memes are tunes, ideas, catch phrases, clothes fashions, ways of making pots or of building arches. Just as genes propagate themselves in the gene pool by leaping from body to body via sperms or eggs, so memes propagate themselves in the meme pool by leaping from brain to brain via a process, which, in the broad sense, can be called imitation. If a scientist hears, or reads about, a good idea, he passes it on to his colleagues and students. He mentions it in his articles and his lectures. If the idea catches on, it can be said to propagate itself, spreading from brain to brain.[7]

Richard Brodie expanded significantly upon Dawkins's work and the science of memetics in his book *Virus of the Mind*. Brodie defines a meme as "a unit of information in a mind whose existence influences events such that more copies of itself get created in other minds." He looks at memes in terms of their "catchiness" and defines the effectiveness of a meme based on how quickly the thought is replicated.[8]

In a very logical fashion, Brodie identifies various categories of memes that function like viruses in the DNA of our various cultures. According to Brodie, memes seem to persist not because of their truth, but because of our individual receptivity to hosting them in our minds.

In my experience, memes are not self-sustaining thought forms that lie dormant in morphic fields as information potential. Rather, memes are active thought-form viruses that thrive by virtue of residing within the mind of the host.

Memes in our minds are not inherently detrimental. Many memes are useful. They enable us to navigate in the world with some semblance of order.

This book defines a meme's effectiveness not in terms of its replicating ability, but in terms of how it assists us practically in living our unlimited potential. Thus, a meme will be defined as being either *useful* and/or *expansive,* or *not useful* and/or *limiting.*

According to Brodie,[9] three predominant types of memes inform our experience:

- Distinction memes
- Strategy memes
- Association memes

Distinction memes

Distinction memes are arbitrary delineations made by labeling and categorizing reality. The state of California is an example of a distinction meme. Knowing your location provides a form of assistance for navigation. While the meme of California is not ultimately true, it is a consistently held construct of consciousness that shapes our behaviors and our experiences. Subsets of distinction memes are associated with California, as well. California has a meme of economics called California sales tax, a meme of language called English, and even a meme called Hollywood that has a multitude of additional, corresponding memes. Change location to another meme, like Mexico, and a completely different set of memes will command your experience, including, but not limited to, country memes, economic memes, cultural memes, social memes, and linguistic memes.[10]

Universal consciousness is all-inclusive and void of distinctions in its undifferentiated nature. Universal consciousness does not make a distinction between California, Washington, Mexico, Europe, and Egypt, or anywhere else, for that matter. These distinction memes are arbitrary lines drawn in the sand which, when followed, command a specific set of experiences within a particular reality. No matter where you draw the line in the sand, it is all still sand.

Strategy memes

Strategy memes, according to Brodie, encode for beliefs relating to cause and effect.[11] They, too, help us to navigate from point A to point B. In this frame of reference, it is a given that if you take certain steps, you will experience a certain outcome.

Examples of *useful* strategy memes include driving a car, cooking, and earning a college degree. Within each respective experience, various steps are employed to accomplish desired objectives. Strategy memes are extremely useful for organizing consciousness in a predictable manner and in a way that facilitates accomplishment of specific goals.

Sometimes strategy memes can limit our experience. For example, at a young age we may encode that not speaking our perceived truth is the only way to fit in or be accepted. Instead, we might choose to say *only* what we think another person wants to hear. Perhaps, then, we make the choice to say nothing at all. So, we develop a strategy meme to deny self-expression or to thwart what we are genuinely thinking or feeling so that we may be accepted by others.

It is common to develop strategy memes as a result of interactions with our parents or guardians.

Imagine that a child, seeing an overweight person, announces loudly and in public that the person is really, really fat. The parents, themselves feeling mortified and embarrassed, punish the child harshly for blurting out this innocent observation. The child is told he is *bad,* and he believes he is *bad* for behaving this way. Thus, a strategy meme is seeded and begins to grow. To mitigate fear and shame, and to avoid future punishment or judgment, the child perpetuates his strategy to *stay safe* by keeping his mouth shut and by quieting both his observations and his perceived truths.

The child may adopt any number of strategy memes that are not unlike our own:

"I will be punished or judged if I speak my truth."

"My observations are not valid or worthy of being heard."

"I should ignore what I see or not observe it at all."

"It is not okay to be honest for fear of being misunderstood, judged, ridiculed, or punished."

Consider children who are programmed with the strategy meme "Be seen and not heard" as a means of parental control. In response to this viral meme, incidental strategy memes develop. These strategies may serve to further support and/or contradict the initial "Be seen and not heard" programming.

We may enter into adolescence and easily succumb to peer pressure while trying desperately to fit in. Years of shunting authentic personal expression may lead to engaging in high-risk behaviors, like sexual promiscuity and drug dependency, in an attempt to gain acceptance.

We enter adulthood with these strategy memes, and life is not as we expected. We may continue to avoid articulating our honest thoughts and feelings to others, and subsequently, not get our fundamental relational needs met. Buried deep within our psyche are the strategy memes that helped us cope or supposedly kept us safe, but those old memes are now worn and tattered like a jacket six sizes too small. Perhaps these habitual ways of behaving have left us feeling like outcasts, feeling like we don't belong anywhere. Perhaps we watch other people go after their dreams, engage in fulfilling relationships, and make their mark in the world while we don't even know what our truth might be. All the while, we are running obsolete, debilitating strategy tapes round and round in our minds, producing limiting programs that create the tapestry (tapes-try) of dysfunctional lives.

Many strategy memes that carry forth into adulthood can and eventually will express as disease. Consider a woman who, for decades, denies her authentic self-expression. She never speaks her mind or shares her feelings in intimate relationships or social settings because of a deeply ingrained strategy meme that commands otherwise. She marries a verbally abusive husband who likes the *idea* of her, based on her presenting strategy meme. At work, she doesn't ever get recognized for a promotion. Her kids manipulate her to get what they want, and her few friends are more like acquaintances or strangers. Eventually, she may develop breast cancer, an auto-immune disorder, or hypothyroidism.

Disease (dis-ease) or a debilitating condition might express itself as a potent placeholder to capture her attention. All those years of unexpressed truths, thoughts, ideas, dreams, and emotions that are contained and resonating in her body can and will eventually beckon recognition. Conceivably, any disease or imbalance is an invitation to recondition a constricted state into a different, more empowering configuration. Within the perceived gift of disease lies the opportunity to dismantle a malignant strategy meme and develop a new, more useful approach to growth and authentic expression. Change your strategy, and you change the course of your life.

Perhaps an important difference between a useful strategy meme and one that is not useful is our degree of self-identification with it. For example, when we are driving a car, we know that we are not the strategy meme; we are simply using a vehicle to transport us from one location to another. However, when we personalize a strategy meme to the extent that we

identify strongly with it, seeing it as a part of our perceived being, then the meme's resonant expression can
limit us.

For instance, some people think they are naturally
shy, when in fact *shy* is a strategy meme adopted in
childhood because of a perceived negative stressor.
Maybe they were humiliated at a party or in school.
Perhaps this non-useful strategy meme was implement-
ed to avoid future embarrassment or rejection. A distinction meme is first created by a person who states, "I am
shy." The strategy becomes "If I am shy, I don't have to
be vulnerable in social circumstances." Rather than
recognizing the strategy for what it is, the person
continually identifies with being shy instead of recognizing *shy* as a patterned choice. *Shy,* or behaving shyly, can
be a strategy for navigating safely in social situations.

Recognition of this meme can liberate a person from
his or her shy behavior by creating space between the
self as I AM and the memetic program *shy* that serves as
a mask for a person's awareness. Creating a new strategy meme, such as, "I am comfortable in my own skin in
social circumstances," or "I am easily able to speak my
thoughts and feelings to others," can allow for a new
pattern of consciousness to habituate and then manifest
into experience.

Association memes

Association memes are memes that have been conceptually fused (con-fused) in our awareness. They are a bit
like attitudes in that the presence of one meme triggers a
thought or an emotion or another meme.[12]

For example, imagine that you had a really mean,
scary teacher in elementary school, one who made you
cry. Let's say that she always wore shirts with green
triangles and red polka dots. As an adult, every time you
see a green-triangle shirt with red polka dots on it, you
feel afraid and sad. That would be considered an associ-

ation meme, because the presence of a shirt patterned like that would be unconsciously *associated,* or linked, with fear and grief.

Advertisers love to use association memes to drive consumer behavior. Their approach is to appeal to our emotions (mostly fears) while insidiously implying that their product will alleviate perceived, unmet needs. Advertisers use association memes to prey upon our vulnerabilities. Some of the most surreptitious advertising is contained in pharmaceutical campaigns. The direct-to-consumer market for prescription drugs is a multibillion dollar market.[13]

As a former pharmaceutical executive for several major drug companies, I can disclose that the advertising strategies of many pharmaceutical companies are not about sharing honest information. Instead, they make exaggerated use of association memes and condense them into a very small amount of time, so that by the end of any given drug commercial, you are programmed to "Ask your doctor if Brand Z is right for you."

Consider a television ad for a name-brand prescription medication that is indicated for treatment of depression. Depression is a distinction meme that has evolved into a morphic field, as we will soon see.

In the beginning of the ad, a series of association memes are utilized to *paint the picture* of a typical depressed patient. Normally, there is an association meme depicted by a typical patient-profile that is designed to appeal to the largest potential target market. For depression, the patient profile is generally that of a female of perimenopausal age. This is *not* done because these women are more likely to be depressed. Instead, it is because these women are presumed to be more vulnerable and calculably more receptive to proactively seeking treatment from a doctor.

The television commercial begins in black and white as opposed to standard Technicolor. The room is dark, and we see a giant *shadow* following the woman. This shadow represents "her depression." Depression itself is personified as a distinction meme and is further mimetically associated with the shadow. A few scenes flash in black and white, which depict her ignoring her family and friends, behaving listlessly, and aimlessly wandering long, dark, narrow hallways with no windows or doors. Okay, so we get the idea. This is her experience of living with "her depression."

The ad may even matter-of-factly disclose that *depression hurts* so that we can also associate pain with depression.

Depression hurts is a new meme that is being created to exploit the relatively untapped market and giant morphic field of *pain*. The distinction meme of *pain* is cleverly associated with depression specifically so we will treat our *pain* with anti-depressants.

Enter *RX Deprexa* (or whatever the drug being promoted is called), and we witness an obvious and somewhat immediate relief from depression, pain, and whatever else was lurking in the *shadows*.

Immediately, the commercial switches to vibrant Technicolor, and we see the same woman joyfully riding her bike through a sunny meadow with her happy, handsome husband, two beautiful, mature teenagers, and her beloved golden retriever. Even the dog is smiling. The woman invariably ends the commercial by exclaiming a crafty association meme such as, "Thanks to Deprexa, I got my life back! Ask *your* doctor if Deprexa is right for *you*."

By the time the commercial is over, the average viewer barely remembers the rapidly mentioned, exceptionally long list of serious side effects. There is only one reason for advertising to make any mention of side effects: because the Federal Trade Commission requires all drug companies to provide what is called *fair balance* in commercials. This means that advertisers must commit equal time to the drug's features, advantages, and benefits and to the associated risks and side effects. I can share with you that there are no such things as *side effects* from pharmaceutical medications. Side effects are the all-inclusive effects of the medications, albeit decidedly inconvenient ones.

However, when warnings are conveniently positioned in between pleasant association memes such as freedom, happiness, and family harmony, very few people acknowledge the risks.

What's interesting is that depression is not truly a disease, although pharmaceutical companies beg to differ. Depression is an experience, one that can be perceived either simply or in a complicated manner. Depression is perhaps only complicated when there is an oversimplified, generalized medical approach that chooses to treat everyone similarly, with similar pharmaceuticals.

Depression appears to be a habituated pattern of consciousness; it is a separation, denial, and/or awareness of perceiving aspects of ourselves in the gap between what we truly are and who we think we need to be. Whether it is simple or complicated may depend upon the path chosen to embrace the recognition, as well as allowance for the gap to close. Regardless, transforming the gaps and grooves of depression is not to be found by looking at the synapses of the brain, nor is depression *healed* through the mask of drug treatment. Drugs are bandages, forms of bondage that create dependency rather than offering us the freedom to realize our infinite potential.

We can reconfigure depression by looking at the whole person and reconnecting fragmented aspects of their awareness. Drugs have their place and can support the process, but they cannot *heal* what is not really broken. There is no hole in whole.

The blatant manipulation that takes place in advertising through the use of association memes can be rendered largely ineffective when we employ our keen awareness. We don't have to be influenced by commercials. As with all programming, we can change the channel. Just change the channel.

Memes of secondary gain

Be aware of secondary gain. Often within strategy memes and association memes are secondary gains with which we are resonating at the conscious or, more likely, unconscious level. We may find that continuing to run a program in a certain way enables us to perceivably gain something in exchange.

During a seminar, a woman approached me and asked if heart-centered awareness would "take care" of all her physical problems. Essentially, I replied that reality is as flexible and malleable as our consciousness allows it to be.

The woman went on to inform me that she was awaiting a large monetary settlement from her insurance company from an accident in which she was involved. In other words, she needed to stay in pain so she could provide documentation from her doctor—so she could receive her reward.

She was running a strategy meme to remain in pain, and it was supported by an association meme that said, "Being in pain provides monetary gain." Her pain was literally a pay in (*pa-in*) for the potential *pay*out or reward that seemed too good to give up.

How often do we postpone transforming something because of the secondary gain we think we'll receive from not allowing change? What if we let go now into a settlement that is not settling at all? What if we allow change to occur in such a way that the reward is centered within us, and from that space, all is provided to us? Of course, secondary gain is usually not as blatant as this example.

I have found that when the secondary gain is removed from a pattern, the pattern naturally falls away. When we don't *pa-in* attention to the secondary gain, or we remove it or replace it with an equally rewarding meme, the old pattern has a chance to change. Pay attention to secondary gains. Paying attention can make the difference between being run by a strategy meme and running a strategy of your own that is associated with change.

Memes as patterns

In ME, we play with memes as patterns of information. We have found that there are personal, social, and global memes that can limit us. We identify these memes and then replace them with more useful, more expansive memes. We have identified several categories of memes, universal in nature, that either *hinder us* or *help us* gain access to our full consciousness potential.

As individuals, we are limited predominantly by parental, intellectual, emotional, social, relational, and survival memes. Common distinction memes, which often have strategy and association memes affiliated with them, include but are not limited to

- Not good enough
- Don't deserve
- Programmed to re-create problem
- Programmed for pain, sickness, disease
- Programmed not to accept help
- Programmed for guilt

Examples of useful corollary memes to the above limiting memes are

- Will to Create
- Will to Accept
- Will to Love
- Will to Learn

- Will to Change
- Will to Forgive

Whether we perpetuate memes often depends upon our naive acceptance of their perceived truth. Memes count on us to host their parties. We keep memes alive in our minds, not because they are true or because we believe them, but because we do not challenge their untruths, and because we do not choose to *not* believe them.

The reality of limiting memes is that, ultimately, they simply do not reflect the truth of who we really are. Truly, none of the limiting memes is actually true. This means that any limiting meme we are running in our personal-perspective reality can be effectively challenged, unraveled, and dismantled. Through awareness, we can trance-form and trance-end any meme of limitation to a meme of expansion.

R-meme-ber, you can choose!

Memes may begin as thoughts in our mind that others copy. It is my experience that when memes become sufficiently replicated, or become deeply contained in our awareness, they form morphic fields. To me, memes appear as nested morphic units. It is curious to ponder the level of critical threshold required for a meme to replicate, habituate, or take shape as a morphic field. I've often contemplated what it takes for a meme to become a morphic field.

Our resonance with limiting memes often ties us into existing global morphic fields of limitation. For example, limiting memes such as fear, anger, resentment, jealousy and frustration (all derivatives of *fear*) connect us in resonance with the global morphic field of *fear*.

When we tap into memes of expansion, such as *will to love, will to learn, will to create,* and *will to accept* (all derivatives of *love*), we are tapping into gargantuan global morphic fields of *love*. This establishes resonance with fields of possibilities that flow through us as waves from the sea of unlimited potential. These expansive memes, and their corresponding morphic fields, are most similar to the essence of that which is universal consciousness as unconditional love, experiencing itself through us.

Morphic fields and memes are neither positive nor negative. Rather, they are simply how consciousness organizes itself. As constructs of universal consciousness, morphic fields and memes are similar in that their operation is based on resonance. While morphic fields become more powerful with awareness, memes become more powerful through lack of awareness. The more aware we are of a morphic field, the more information we contribute to it, and ultimately the more powerful and conscious it becomes.

Conversely, the more unaware we are of the limiting memes we resonate with, the more those memes limit us. Fortunately, we can unravel the limiting memes that restrain us and create new memes that allow us to expand into more of our unlimited potential. Similarly, through awareness, we can choose which limiting morphic fields to disentangle from and choose new, more expansive, more useful morphic field resonances.

Practical Play: Unravel and Reveal

Unravel and Reveal shows us how to disentangle from limiting memes that restrain us and create new memes that allow us to expand into more of our unlimited potential.

- Grab a pen or pencil and paper.
- Think of something you know about yourself that you would like to change. For example, "I want a new job."
- Write down any thoughts, ideas, images, doodles, or stories that come to mind.

- Ask the open-ended question, "If I knew what memes were operating in my mind to prevent me from experiencing my desired change, what comes to mind?"
- Write down any thoughts, ideas, images, doodles, or stories that come to mind.
- Ask yourself, "Is what I have written, drawn, or thought about true?"
- Write down any thoughts, ideas, or images that occur to you affirming that what you scribed is *not* true.
- Ask yourself, "What part(s) of this meme, if any, is true *or* seems to be true?"
- Write down any thoughts, ideas, images, doodles, or stories that come to mind.
- Ask yourself, "Is this true?" Write down any thoughts that occur to you affirming that it is *not* true. Hint: It is never true unless you make it true. Any perceived limitation is a meme.
- Ask yourself if what you scribed is a distinction meme, a strategy meme, or an association meme?
- Write down any thoughts, ideas, images, doodles, or stories that come to mind.
- Separate the concepts. Example: Let's suppose that the limiting meme preventing a desired new job from manifesting is, "I can't do work that I love and make money at it." This is an example of a distinction meme, a strategy meme, and an association meme. It's a triple whammy!
- Simplify the memes by separating the words that you wrote down, like this:

  I can't
  Work
  Love
  Money

- Ask yourself, "If I knew where this meme was first created, what might show up?" You may remember your father giving up his dream to be a writer and taking a job as an electrician to *provide* for the family. The meme "I can't do what I love and make money" could have been encoded at an early age out of fears about security. If the meme no longer suits you, *just choose* a different, more useful one. Invite awareness to release the resonance with the limiting or no-longer-useful meme and return the pattern back to universal consciousness to be reconfigured as personal potential that is more empowering.

- Now, ask yourself, "If I were to begin resonating with a more useful meme, one that would enable me to easily manifest this change, what comes to mind?" Feel free to leverage the useful memes provided earlier in this chapter.
- Write down any thoughts, ideas, images, doodles, or stories that come to mind.
- Notice how you feel when you write down the new, expansive meme. What positive emotions do you associate with this meme?
- Write down any thoughts, ideas, images, doodles, or stories that come to mind.
- After replacing the limiting meme with a meme that facilitates your desired objective, ask yourself, "If I knew where this new, useful meme wants to be "installed" in my personal field or physical body, where does my awareness go? It may be your left arm or your throat or your chest or your heart. Wherever your awareness goes, trust it, and literally or figuratively place the new, useful meme there.
- Now, as before, notice what is different, not what is the same.

The key with this Practical Play is to remain curious and aware of the memes that may be like *shadows* lurking in your path. When you reflect upon them through your awareness, most likely you will see that you are not your *shadows*. Rather, you are the light that shines upon them.

Containers for Consciousness and Choice

Morphic fields and memes are vehicles by which universal consciousness organizes and expresses information, light, and resonance from formless nothingness, to information potentials, to actuality. Morphic fields, in particular, serve as self-organizing vehicles or containers in which consciousness experiences itself. They give shape to information. Morphic fields maintain form and order, extending from a formless and order-less medium to inform the behavior of anyone or anything that resonates with them.

Morphic fields and memes are organized forms of information that can either expand or limit our experiences. Perhaps we sometimes may not perceive choices as being available because we are consciously or unconsciously in resonance with a morphic field or meme that is *seemingly* doing the choosing for us. We *do* have the power, as a direct extension of universal consciousness, to choose our own resonance. We can change the channel. Not only that, we can change the channel whenever or however we choose. Where we choose to resonate or where we choose to connect to grids of information gives shape and form to our experiences.

Scientific discoveries and observations of human behavior have demonstrated that we have the ability to modify our resonance with specific fields of information or programs to change our experiences.

Yes, we can choose to modify our resonance with specific fields to change our experiences.

Yes, we can dismantle limiting memes and create new, more expansive memes.

We can choose. You can choose. Just choose.

FOUR

Matrix Energetics
Possibilities and Play

Do nothing; leave nothing undone.
> —*Lao Tzu,* Tao Te Ching

Do nothing and leave nothing undone: this is at the core of what we teach our students to do for themselves in ME.

Why would anyone want to learn how to do nothing? Because when we do nothing, we gain access to all that is consciousness potential.

When we teach doing nothing, as in we are not the *doer*, we become an open door for grace to work through us. We do no-thing and get out of the way, while still engaging as active participants *and* not as separate beings, trying to make something happen. We become antennae for a chosen field, an extension of its potential, leveraging our awareness as a platform of possibility states for anything we might encounter.

ME is a morphic field that was deliberately engineered to be a fertile playground for miracles and rapid transformation. It is based on the holographic principles of light, information, and resonance. Remember, we are made of light, and we interact and resonate with information holographically. What unfolds and is expressed from this empowering connection is energy and experience.

Practically speaking, the holographic principles embedded in a morphic field allow for any pattern of consciousness to change, even if we do not direct our intention to it.

While it is not necessary to understand holographic theory to derive benefit from a morphic field, understanding the nature of a hologram enables us to be more receptive to how its effects reverberate through us.

What Is a Hologram?

According to American Author Michael Talbot,

> a hologram is a three-dimensional photograph made with the aid of a laser. To make a hologram, the object to be photographed is first bathed in the light of a laser beam. Then a second laser beam is bounced off the reflected light of the first and the resulting interference pattern (the area where the two laser beams commingle) is captured on film. When the film is developed, it looks like a meaningless swirl of light and dark lines. But as soon as the developed film is illuminated by another laser beam, a three-dimensional image of the original object appears. The three-dimensionality of such images is not the only remarkable characteristic of holograms. If a hologram of a rose is cut in half and then illuminated by a laser, each half will still be found to contain the entire image of the rose. Indeed, even if the halves are divided again, each snippet of film will always be found to contain a smaller but intact version of the original image. Unlike normal photographs, every part of a hologram contains all the information possessed by the whole.[1]

Understanding holograms enabled some physicists to understand the seemingly bizarre behavior of electrons that were thousands of miles apart and yet were able to communicate with each other instantly. Physicists discovered that communication between electrons traveled faster than the speed of light, regardless of the distance traveled. Theoretical physicist David Bohm concluded that this instant communication was possible because the electrons were not separate, at all.[2] Rather, they only appeared to be separate.

Bohm's theory postulates that "at a deeper level of reality all things in the universe are infinitely interconnected . . . reality is a sort of superhologram in which the past, present, and future all exist simultaneously."[3]

Holographically, we are not separate, nor do the sum of our parts equal our whole. To be precise, each of our parts contains all the information that is encoded in the totality of our being. Therefore, when we change the configuration of a knee or a hip, the change connects us to all the patterns of light and information that resonate in our personal field, which comprises the totality of our experience of reality. In other words nothing happens in a vacuum. Change one thing, and everything can change.

Connecting our personal fields with the holographic templates of unlimited potential embedded in certain morphic fields creates transformative experiences that continue without limitation.

ME is based on *what is possible,* as opposed to what is *not* possible. As we have previously learned, morphic fields appear to function based on memories and habits. As defined by Dr. Sheldrake, morphic fields function based on the information that is encoded within the individual holons or morphic units encoded in the field, thus giving rise to form and experience.[4]

It is morphic field resonance that organizes and commands much of our experience in our personal fields. When we tap into a field of miracles and transformation, then miracles as transformation are more likely to occur.

According to Rupert Sheldrake,

> if it is easier to learn things that many people have learned before, educational methods that enhance the process of morphic resonance could lead to accelerated learning and more effective educational methods.[5]

As such, there are some very practical applications for learning and *unlearning* that can be facilitated by leveraging the awareness within morphic fields.

Knowing that morphic fields function based on memory, the consciousness technology known as ME was intentionally built as a morphic field so that it would facilitate *easy* learning for all who chose to connect with it. Tens of thousands of students and practitioners have tapped into the morphic field of ME in the past decade, which has accelerated the learning process. People are able to quickly access this method of interactive reality-creation because the information in the morphic field is available and readily accessible.

With the relative contribution of each student, a natural feedback loop occurs. Inevitably, as a morphic field receives, it gives. A morphic field gets stronger and more self-aware the more we play in its potential. Again, because the individual contribution of each student amplifies the strength of the morphic field, learning ME has become progressively effortless over the past several years.

What Matrix Energetics Is

So, what is ME? We choose not to define it because what is being defined then becomes limited in expression, based upon the parameters set forth in its description. How we define anything creates the construct or container through which information can disseminate. Thus, we declare that we do not know what ME *is*, however we do know what it *does*.

Here is how we sometimes describe it: ME is a powerful field of consciousness potential that supports instantaneous and lifelong transformation for physical, mental, emotional, spiritual, relational, financial, environmental, and self-referential patterns.

Based upon widely known principles of quantum physics and lesser-known principles of torsion physics, ME taps into the morphic field of infinite potential and provides easy access to limitless possibilities. There are no prerequisites for learning ME other than curiosity and a willingness to play.

I consider the field of ME is a field of grace and playfulness that celebrates, "Come just as you are and leave transformed." The field mirrors back to us that which is our true essence, which is light, which is love and a coherent expression of universal consciousness.

Okay, so what exactly is ME? Instead of describing its multitude of characteristics and tendencies, it may be more useful to define ME by what it is *not*.

- ME is not a technique.
- ME is not "running energy" or doing energy work.
- ME is not a cult or an exclusive group of people.
- ME is not whatever you think it is based on what you already think you know.

Matrix Energetics is not a technique

The only thing ME has in common with a technique is that most techniques work through morphic resonance. Techniques are ritualized methods of noticing and interacting with information to create specific outcomes. One must follow the steps of the techniques in a processed, habituated fashion for them to work.

Conversely, ME has no specific steps for creating specific outcomes. Students are taught to trust what shows up in the moment and to let go of all attachments to specific outcomes. ME is a consciousness technology that is both completely adaptive and totally flexible.

Martial Artist Bruce Lee had three basic tenets:

- Absorb what is useful.
- Discard what is not.
- Add what is uniquely your own.

In ME, these tenets have been adopted and adapted:

- Absorb what is useful.
- Discard the classical mess.
- No way as way.

It is a kind of mantra that reminds us to notice what we notice, jettison the limitations of prior training and self-limiting perceptual biases, and get out of the way so the field can flow through us as spontaneous expression.

In the field of ME, we do not treat disease (dis-ease). We treat people. We embrace each person as a unique configuration of light, information, and resonance. There exists a flexibility of consciousness within the field of ME that permits a reconfiguration of individual awareness and a change in resonance. Change the resonance, and the experience changes.

A key to recognizing change is to notice what is different versus what is the same. This is a fundamental principle in ME that is based on the nature of change and the ability to access infinite potential. This mantra is useful because it does not tell us *what* to notice, or *how* to notice, or *where* to notice. The art of noticing is unique to each individual. This construct encourages us to establish resonance with new and different patterns of information that express as different experiences.

While ME is not a technique, we do provide methods for noticing and interacting with information in the field. We provide strategies for navigating through terrains of consciousness reliably and consistently, including, but not limited to, the Two Point, Time Travel, Parallel Universes, Archetypes, 21 Frequencies, Windows, Modules, and Templates. These tools, and many more, serve as maps for navigating through a limitless playground of potential. These constructs offer some semblance of structure and a process for organizing awareness in the morphic field of ME for exploring unlimited consciousness. They are ways to navigate the virtual maps of consciousness, making it easier to traverse the territory, but they are not the territory.

When we teach, we provide suggestions that help us get out of the way so that the field can work through us. How that occurs is unique for every person. Perhaps this is why ME is so immensely popular. The field is not interested in creating a group of automatons. The field invites everyone to express himself or herself uniquely. "No way as way." This means that there is no right way or wrong way to experience or do ME.

Matrix Energetics is not running energy or doing energy work

What is energy? It has been defined as "the ability (or capacity) to do work."

So, energy work is the capacity to do work as work.

Consequently, running energy is running the capacity to do work, which is tiring and laborious. Models that are based on running energy are limited because they are closed systems, and closed systems require the practitioner to transfer energy to something or to someone or to somewhere. Usually, there are only finite domains for energy to transfer into. This is why running energy is so exhausting! Burnout is common whenever we run energy.

ME, as a morphic field, is an open system and an informational field that functions holographically through resonance. Practically speaking, what this means is that we connect to packets of information as if they were seeds of awareness. When we connect to them, the packet opens and what unfolds is expressed as energy. Energy is the result of connecting to the information, but it is not the source of the experience. There is no running energy when playing in the field of ME. There is only accessing limitless packets of holographic information, establishing resonance, and allowing for new expressions.

Matrix Energetics is not a cult or an exclusive group of people

By its very nature, a cult conditions and controls the behavior of its members. ME is a non-local morphic field that is available for deprogramming limiting grids of awareness so as to free us from our perceived limitations. Most cults require belief in a mission and demand unopposed admiration of and devotion to its principles. Belief in the field of ME is not required; it will work, anyway. Objectively, it does not care what you think. ME knows you are more than your thoughts, your beliefs, and your prior limiting experiences. There is nothing to cling onto in ME. The field is about freedom and flexibility in consciousness and about perceiving the world with innocent perception.

Matrix Energetics is not whatever you think it is based on what you already think you know

Some who encounter ME have a tendency to compare it to what they already think they know. ME is not what you think based on what you already know. Some who are new to ME mistakenly claim that it's like running energy or like pumping chi or like reiki. When we encounter something new or something outside of our reference frame, we tend to associate it with something familiar so we can better understand it. We try to find in it a resonance that is similar to something we already know so we can comfortably organize it in our awareness. And, if we look for similarities with what we already know, we will discover them. Instead, practice noticing what is different, not what is the same. What this means is that we are capable of expanding our lenses of perception *if* we are willing to expand the apertures of our awareness to consciously move into experiencing this field.

ME is whatever we want it to be. Simple. Just like tofu, that flexibly absorbs flavors, the ME field will conform its expression to individual preferences. After several years engaging with ME, my experience is that the field has a desire to play with us so that we can explore and experience more of ourselves as holographic reflections of unlimited consciousness.

Matrix Energetics, Morphic Fields, and Memes

In the teachings of ME, we pay close attention to morphic fields and memes. We learn how to quickly and easily identify morphic fields with which we are resonating with, as well as the memes that are empowering and/or limiting us so that we can choose how to modify our resonance. Through conscious awareness, we then are able to disconnect from any programs or patterns that limit us and consciously connect to different grids of information that will empower us. We are readily able to disengage from anything we no longer choose to resonate with. We no longer need to resonate with limiting programs, limiting beliefs, or even limiting morphic fields and memes. We are able to effortlessly engage in an entirely new way of being based on our essence as limitless beings. We are able to experience the truth of who we are as universal consciousness with all our inherent infinite potential.

Tapping into a morphic field of consciousness potential such as ME is not a prescription for bliss or for a life free from problems. Is that possible? Perhaps. Is it probable or likely? Perhaps. Bliss and perfection can take on a completely different meaning when we expand awareness to resonate with universal consciousness and unlimited potentials as options. Establishing a connection to any empowering, expansive, useful morphic field provides choices, options, and expanded templates for awareness. These allow us to navigate practically through patterns of information. All we have to do is choose.

Playing with consciousness technologies like ME offers a useful prescription for expanded perception, which allows for limitless potentials to manifest as experience. We learn that problems are patterns, and patterns are placeholders for our awareness to move into greater recognition of choosing different options. This is not positive thinking. This is flexibility of consciousness.

Problems as Patterns as Placeholders

What is intended by the statement, "Problems are patterns, and patterns are placeholders for our awareness?" The dictionary defines a problem as "a matter or situation regarded as unwelcome or harmful and needing to be dealt with and overcome." A problem is perceived as something *being in the way,* and it has a predominately negative connotation, along with limited associations that restrict our options. On a polarity scale, a problem gets a *negative charge.* Unknown solutions for any identified problems would sit on the opposite end of the polarity scale, yielding a corresponding *positive charge.* Unfortunately, as long as we are attempting to focus on finding a solution for *a problem,* we are still resonating with its polarity, which is *the problem.*

Albert Einstein allegedly said, "No problem can be solved from the same level of consciousness that created it." This implies that we must transcend our limited awareness of the problem, which is the same resonant awareness that created it and subsequently labeled it, and access a different resonance of possibilities from a more expanded consciousness.

Labeling problems as patterns allows us to move awareness into neutral territory. Furthermore, it provides us with wiggle room for the pattern to reconfigure.

Interacting with a *pattern* rather than a *problem,* a *condition,* or a *disease* also frees any pattern from its morphic and memetic resonance with other similar patterns.

Defining disease in-forms disease

Let us explore the naming of a disease. Initially, the name itself is only a label. The label is a distinction meme. The label stems from a conglomeration of signs and symptoms that have been separated through distinctions, identified, and then connected again in association with each other through assigning a name or a diagnosis. This distinction meme has corresponding limiting strategy memes, as well as references that form association memes around a developing pattern. So, while a label initially seems benign as a distinction meme, it soon forms association memes coupled with corresponding strategy memes, which are known as *treatments*. These nested memes address the original signs and symptoms. Such powerful, influential programs give shape to the resonant expression of the morphic field of a defined disease by virtue of the information encoded in the morphic units that are mimetically linked together.

Labels limit us

Consider a diagnosis of cancer. A diagnosis of cancer, which is created from a conglomerate of memetic signs and symptoms, is initially a problem and then becomes a disease. Cancer is an association meme that resonates with the corresponding morphic field of cancer. The ever-expanding morphic field of cancer includes all of the patients who have ever been diagnosed with cancer and all of the doctors who have ever treated cancer or been trained to look for it.

The morphic field also includes all of the pharmaceutical companies who have diligently invested time, research, and millions of dollars into creating a market for this disease to capture patients eligible for potential or existing drug treatments. Let us not forget that the morphic field of cancer also includes various cancer charities that are "raising awareness" of cancer. Focus is invested in raising funds for a cure all the while continually reminding us of cancer by encouraging everyone to wear pink bows and yellow wristbands. Cancer is not a *can-cure*.

Cancer is a morphic field of disease that gets bigger the more we focus our awareness on it. When we focus on disease, we amplify the morphic field and morphic resonance. When we focus on a cure for a disease, we are still focused on the *dis-ease*.

Diseases are nothing more than engineered morphic fields. To unplug from resonances with specific grids of information, it is quite helpful to disengage from the diagnostic label (i.e., cancer, diabetes, asthma, high blood pressure, depression, anxiety, obesity). Labels limit us. When a disease, diagnosis, or condition is finally realized as a pattern, then wiggle room for transformation ensues.

In ME we do not treat disease. We treat people who are unique configurations of light, information, and resonance. Patterns are the language of potentials, and when we modify the resonance with the patterns, through awareness, then transformation flows naturally.

Matrix Energetics: Reflections of Wonder

The field of ME is a house of mirrors that reflecting back to us a more liberated awareness of our limiting patterns, perceptions, beliefs, programs, and thoughts so we can shift into something different, more expansive, and certainly more useful.

As we disentangle from our limiting patterns, perceptions, beliefs, programs, and thoughts, we return to creative thinking, and therein is where curiosity becomes our greatest teacher. The field truly responds to curiosity. The less you think you know and the more curious you become, the more the field will respond to you.

Consider the question: "I wonder what it would be like if . . . ?" Ask this question with a child's innocent perception and curiosity and notice where your awareness takes you.

Tapping into miracles

When writing the second ME book, *The Physics of Miracles,* the decision was made to proceed with that title specifically to establish a morphic resonance. Presumably, if more people become aware of the physics of miracles, then miracles will inevitably become more frequent. The field itself seems to recognize that everything, every moment, is a miracle unfolding. In fact, for many people, it appears there is no difference between a miracle and a process, except for the illusion of time. So, why wait? Notice now that the gift of a miracle is the present. Open it.

What is a miracle? It is defined as "an extraordinary event manifesting divine intervention in human affairs; an extremely outstanding or unusual event, thing, or accomplishment."

I define a miracle as anything that occurs that is outside the realm of expectation or beyond a preconceived notion of what is a likely occurrence for an outcome. When we let go of expectations, preconceived notions, and attachments to specific outcomes, every moment becomes miracle. When we expect the unexpected, the unexpected becomes the new normal. Miracles are the expressions of consciousness potential through us, as us. We are the technology of miracles; we are the physics of miracles; and it is all easily accessible when we connect to a morphic field of potentiality, such as ME.

The field sees us as it sees itself, as part of the whole, divinely inspired, and perfect exactly as we are. Upon recognition of our core essence, diseases and problems often disappear, along with the confusion, imbalance, and patterned perceptions that created them. The awareness of our divine spark, even if only witnessed for a moment, evokes a process of transformation that some would call a miracle. Awareness says, "I see you as the Divine sees you. I experience you as the Divine experiencing itself. I know that you are love because that is all I am, and we are the same in everything."

Practical Play: Unlocking a Space for Grace and Miracles

A key to unlocking a space for grace and miracles is to not put any limits on the universe. That includes not defining how a miracle shows up, or what it looks like. It may be a miracle when an illness disappears, but so is having a parking space open up right in front of you.

- Invite a miracle into your life. Ask yourself, "What if a miracle occurred?" The question is an invitation, like a pebble dropped into the field of possibility. Avoid holding any ideas of what your miracle will be or how it will show up. Rather, extend the invitation and trust that it will unfold.
- At the end of the day, take a look at any events that could have been a response to your invitation. Was there a moment that felt like an answer to your open-ended question? Were there several moments?
- Cultivate a sense of noticing the miraculous in every moment by realizing that a series of successive miraculous moments cradled consistently in your awareness establishes a new state, a new state that, when nurtured long enough, becomes a new, magnificent reality.

FIVE

Heart-Centered Awareness
Portal to Joy

When we move from comparative logic to heart centered unity we find whole new possibilities for perceiving and predicting experiences for our lives. Perhaps all our limitations in life are rooted in limited perspectives about life.
—*Glenda Green,* Keys to Jeshua

The field of the heart provides us with direct access to our inner voice, our inner wisdom, and our inner chamber of limitless potential. The field of the heart creates a coherent connection with universal consciousness. There are no limitations when accessing the field of the heart, and similarly, there are no limitations to the infinite methods or strategies for noticing, listening, and speaking from the field of the heart.

When attention takes us to a particular space or place within an individual's field, we are not just interacting with that space or place. We are interacting with information. Consider that everything in the universe is comprised of light, information, and resonance. When we observe a particular space or place, we create resonance with the information embedded within what we notice. It is the very act of observing information in a state of neutrality that provides a vehicle for transformation to occur.

Patterns appear to change when we observe a particular space or place from the field of the heart. We aren't really doing anything in particular, other than observing information. However, the act of observing entangles the observer with the observed, and this facilitates a different resonance with, or expression of, the information.

Information in a pattern may be contained within torsion fields. Torsion fields are thought to exist everywhere in universal consciousness.[1] The field of the heart is a torsion field.[2] It presents like a doughnut comprised of two counter-rotating fields, with the inner torsion spinning in one direction and the outer torsion spinning in the opposite direction. Within these torsion fields, there is a vortex. Within the vortex, information as potential couples with both of the enfolding torsion fields. This creates a certain amount of inertia and momentum simultaneously, which helps the information pop through the vacuum as form, action, and experience. Information (inform-in-action) as possibility creates experience directly from the field of the heart.

The field of the heart is not the actual physical heart, but it includes the physical heart, because the heart field is all-inclusive.

According to research conducted at Institute of HeartMath,

> the heart generates the body's most powerful and most extensive rhythmic electromagnetic field. Compared to the electromagnetic field produced by the brain, the electrical component of the heart's field is about 60 times greater in amplitude, and permeates every cell in the body. The magnetic component is approximately 5000 times stronger than the brain's magnetic field and can be detected several feet away from the body with sensitive magnetometers.[3]

The torsion field of the heart may be one of the very first things that forms, even before the physical heart manifests, and everything emanates from that torsion field. When we access the field of the heart, we access pure potentiality *prior to* that potentiality expressing as form and experience.

All morphic fields can be accessed from the field of the heart. One reason we drop down into the field of the heart is because it allows us to access a state of pure potentiality and neutrality. From the field of the heart, we can access undifferentiated states of information and consciousness potential *before* the information separates into form and defines itself through action, perspective, and or experience. The heart field is the gateway to all that is, and to all that is yet to be experienced.

When we drop down into the field of the heart, we don't usually feel, notice, or think anything at all related to that experience, because it's not an experience, yet. The field of the heart is pure potential. When we engage in interactive reality-creation, we do it from the pure potentiality and neutrality that is the field of the heart. From the field of the heart we have access to an inherent setting that allows transformation to occur, because we are actually accessing a state of being *before* the collapse of the wave function.

We create resonance with a pattern before that pattern has been separated, identified, and named as a particular experience. So when we work with a knee, for example, it's not actually a knee, because a knee is something that has been separated out from the whole, identified as, and then named as a *knee*. Naming this pattern creates corresponding references that limit what is possible for that *knee* because of all the thoughts and beliefs that accompany the preconceived world of *knees* as a kind of *knee-dom*. There is not much freedom in *knee-dom*. But, there is freedom to engage in unlimited choices when we play with *knee* as an unnamed pattern.

When we do not label or name something, it simply becomes a pattern of information. A pattern becomes pure potentiality, and in that statelessness, we gain access to equally weighted possibilities. This approach facilitates the probability of transformation into actuality.

The physics of heart-centered awareness is the same torsion-field physics that supports action at a distance, remote healing, instantaneous healing, time-travel, levitation, invisibility, and unlimited (free) energy. The physics of torsion fields is an emerging model of physics that has been available for thousands of years. It is the physics of us. It is the physics of love.

The Physics of Us

There is utility in having a general idea of the various physics models presented here, as they offer insight into practical aspects of reality-creation. We are addressing some of them in this book to assist us in leveraging our own abilities to create desired changes in our lives.

Understanding the physics provides maps for navigating through patterns of consciousness. Remember, though, the maps are not the territory. Rather, they are models that explain consciousness, and thus they are useful to expand our experience of ourselves as limitless beings.

In addition, understanding the physics enables us to embody an awareness of how we can notice and experience ourselves differently. The physics we address in this book helps us comprehend how change and transformation can happen instantly and how, in the very next moment, life can be different.

Specifically, a general understanding of torsion-field physics further assists us in recognizing our role in consciously connecting to morphic fields and memes. Morphic fields and memes are containers for consciousness, torsion fields of information, which, through resonance, shape and form our individual (and shared) experiences.

Consider the following explanations that leverage certain principles in torsion-field physics and quantum physics, as well as offer simplified descriptions of interactive reality-creation. Furthermore, they shed more light upon the influence that individual perspective plays in creating conscious experience.

We learned in Chapter 2 that light may be the source of life and that all living things, including you and I, are made of biophotons, which are light. We also learned that biophotons create a coherent body hologram, generating torsion fields, while also communicating with torsion fields in the aura.

It was further shared in Chapter 2 that torsion fields appear to be everywhere in the universe and that the communication of information by torsion fields is not limited to space or time. Torsion fields can communicate with other torsion fields anywhere, instantly.

In Chapter 3, we learned that information in universal consciousness is organized in morphic fields, which inform behavioral habits through morphic resonance. Memes also inform and create programmed behavior by transmitting thoughts virally from one person to another. It was postulated that both morphic fields and memes might utilize torsion fields, which are everywhere, as containers for information and communication.

In Chapter 4, we learned that the universe might be a hologram. Nothing is separate and everything is connected. Remember, in a hologram, parts of the hologram contain the whole. So, if the universe is a hologram, we are a hologram.

If we are made of light (biophotons), which we are, and light creates the body hologram that communicates information through torsion fields, and if torsion fields are everywhere, then according to holographic principles, the universe is made of light, information, and torsion fields, too.

Furthermore, in Chapter 2 we discussed universal consciousness and its unlimited potentials. It was stated that universal consciousness is all and that every-thing comes from no-thing, which is undifferentiated consciousness potential. Well, how does nothing become something? How does that which is distinction-less and formless flow into distinction and form?

Torsion as Consciousness Spinning in "Ether" Direction

Physicist Daniel Winter postulates that the answer lies in the ether or non-material substance of the universe. Winter's ether (aether) model, implosion physics, is nicely summarized in Jan Wicherink's informative book, *Souls of Distortion Awakening:*

> Daniel Winter presents a physics model called "implosion physics." He concludes that the entire universe, the material world is created from one non-material substance, the aether. The aether is a kind of super conductive fluid that flows right through all physical objects. The aether vacuum is an extremely dense nonetheless frictionless medium. The best comparison for the aether being non-material in nature is the super conductive state of helium. When helium is cooled down to temperatures below 2 degrees Kelvin it becomes a super-fluid, which means that objects can move through this fluid with no friction at all.[4]

Daniel Winter believes that vortexes, little eddies or tornados in the fluid-like aether, are the basic building blocks of matter. Since the aether is some kind of a fluid, it follows the well-known physical laws of hydrodynamics.[5]

Let's make sure we read that correctly: "little eddies or tornadoes . . . are the basic building blocks of matter." Hmm? A torsion field is an eddy. A torsion field is the shape of a tornado. A torsion field is a torus. The field of the heart is a torus.

> Now the torus is a unique flow form in hydrodynamics; it allows fluids to spiral inwards and outwards on the same surface of the torus. It is a very stable flow form. If the universe is essentially created from one universal substance, the aether, it must be form that is used to create different and separate things out of this universal substance. The torus is nature's perfect flow form to create a

80

seemingly separate entity in the formless aether that is stable enough to last.[6]

According to Winter's model, the torus is the container for consciousness potential to experience itself in form. Torsion fields spin. When spinning, torsion fields multiply. Multiple torsion fields, as vehicles for universal consciousness, nest together, creating what are known as platonic solids or geometric shapes. Depending upon the number of nested torsion fields, the shapes will change, giving rise to different geometric forms. This nesting can continue indefinitely, in an infinite number of fractal patterns that are holonomic expressions.[7]

The implosion model states:

> Matter is the stable flow form pattern emerging from the aether. It takes on geometrical shapes from a formless energy, creating the illusion of separate electron particles in the electron shells and the particles that make up the nucleus.[8]

Winter also maintains that the electrons in the electron shells correspond with the vortexes that are nested in Platonic symmetries. Winter believes the electron *particles* are actually vortex *waveforms*.[9]

For purposes of this book, consider aether (ether) the undifferentiated sea of consciousness potential. The ether as unconditional love *is* this sea of potential without a mechanism for experiencing itself. There appear to be no conditions for love to know itself.

In seeking to know and experience itself, that which is unconditional love, as light, may have begun to dance and spin in its own vibration. That dance of spin may be what created a torsion field, and perhaps subsequent torsion fields are spun from that original spin. Multiple torsion fields nest together, creating reflections and a geometry of coherence, forming a container that love as light can pour itself into to experience itself through the distinctions of unlimited possibilities.

Collapse of the Wave Function and Our Awareness

Collapse of the wave function is a common quantum physics term that stems from the famous double-slit experiment popularized by physicist Richard Feynman. The double-slit experiment demonstrates that matter and energy can display characteristics of both waves and particles.[10]

Simply stated, scientists were interested in exploring the nature of an electron and wanted to determine whether it was a particle or a wave. When they were in the room observing the electron, it behaved as a particle, which conformed to their expectations. When scientists left the room and were not observing the electron, but videotaped the activity, the electron behaved like an indiscriminate wave. Scientists concluded that the expectations of the researchers *collapsed the wave function,* changing it from probable wave states to particle-based fixed forms. They concluded that, indeed, the consciousness of the observer collapses the wave function.

So why are we concerned with what a particle may be doing or whether it is waving or not waving when we are not looking at it? When we understand that our observations and expectations actually influence the apparent behavior of reality, then we are empowered to actively play with interactive reality-creation. Reality is neither particle nor wave. It is both and neither simultaneously, and as co-creators with universal consciousness, we influence how reality shapes itself.

Likewise, in our continual observations of our reality, and ourselves, we repeatedly *collapse the wave function* into a state of *sameness,* or a state of *no-change.* We perceive through the same lens of awareness, and that collapses the wave function from various possibility states into the ones we have chosen to observe for ourselves. Our limited lens of awareness creates perceptual biases that filter what we are able to notice and experience.

How we perceive life is a result of how we collapse wave functions. Our perspectives, our observations, our opinions, our thoughts, and our beliefs are continually collapsing the wave function from unlimited possibilities, to probability states, into what we actually observe and perceive as our experience. We *see* what we expect to see, and we are continually and consistently collapsing the wave function.

When we play in a powerful morphic field, such as ME, it is presumed that we are *uncollapsing* the wave function from a particle-based, fixed, immutable, limited-perspective reality. We are uncollapsing the wave function from a single causal reality, which is a state of no-change with no flexibility, into wave-based states of possibilities or a state of flux.[11] From a wave-based state of flux, we are able to perform what is referred to as a second weak-collapse of the wave function into a new configuration of consciousness, a new state of change. We are able to move from a state of *no-change* with no flexibility, to a state of flux, to a new state of change or transformation.

The collapse of the wave function is what happens when we exercise choice. Consider that the field of consciousness potential is a coherent smear of infinite information and undifferentiated potential. Consciousness potential is all-inclusive and excludes nothing. Out of a coherent, undifferentiated infinite field, which is much like a motionless sea of potential, distinct possibility states well up as waves in the expanse that decoheres from the all into subsets. These subsets remain part of the all, but they have wavelike characteristics that are in motion and can be tracked by the intuitive right brain. From that state of decoherence, these possibility waves become even more probable in that some waves have more density or are more heavily weighted with information. *Possibility waves* that are more densely weighted become *probability states* that are then more likely to collapse. When we allow for choice to enter through the left brain logic frame of the observer, there is a collapse of the wave function from *multiple probable states* into actuality, much like a drop of water coalescing with the sand. Wave transforms into particle, as consciousness, through individual observation, collapses into wave function, and what is noticed is matter, form, and experience.

Collapse of Wave Function and Torsion Fields

As we have learned, torsion fields are everywhere, even in our personal fields.[12]

When we collapse the wave function from possibility to actuality as a defined personal perspective (particle of reality), this particle of electron-perspective has a spin (an angular momentum of perspective). Each perspective or particle spin creates a torsion field in its wake.[13]

An individual perspective, represented and reflected by the wave function collapse, also creates a torsion field that is encoded as part of collective consciousness. As we know, torsion fields can transmit and receive information anywhere at anytime. Thus, our personal perspective creates a torsion field that encodes the information of our *angle* or personal vantage point. This torsion field is then enfolded within the torsion fields of the ether, or the universal fabric of consciousness. Our unique *spin on things* is encoded in the hologram.

Our choices, thoughts, emotions, and consistently held states are available for others to resonate with, through torsion fields. This is perhaps why our personal thoughts, emotions, choices, and resonance can influence the world, which lends exciting understanding to Mahatma Gandhi's famous proclamation, "You must be the change you wish to see in the world."

When we become the change we wish to see, our individual body hologram of light emits torsion fields based on the spin of our particular electrons or personal vantage point. Change the spin, and you change what becomes more likely to occur for you and for the collective consciousness.

Our thoughts, emotions, and choices do not happen in a vacuum; they influence what is expressed from the vacuum of infinite potential. How we collapse the wave function, as well as how we uncollapse the wave function, influences everything, because everything is connected and everything is synchronized through reciprocal torsion-field communication by one, with the all.

Our personal perspectives, which can change in an instant, have an effect that reverberates out to collective consciousness. This ripple effect has no limits in the same way universal consciousness is unlimited in its potential.

Playing in Waves Changes the Tide and Current

Some speculate that an uncollapse of the wave function happens *naturally* when we play. Play puts us in our hearts and enables us to bypass our linear, logical, analytical brain, which constructs reality based on what is familiar. The logical part of the brain compartmentalizes and segregates information. It sorts through information, based on similarities, by categorizing and organizing what it encounters. It notices what is the same, not what is different. This part of our awareness separates, identifies, and names. The linear, logical part of the brain, often referred to as the left brain, is a *serial processor* that is capable of tracking little more than a few bits of information at a time. As such, the left brain maintains order in reality by collapsing the wave function from multiple waves of possibilities into just one choice. Each choice seems to follow the prior choice in a linear, sequential fashion.

The reasoning left brain part of awareness decides what to perceive, based on what it already knows, and then only what is familiar is noticed and subsequently experienced. The left brain appears to be governed by a separative, particle-based reality. The left brain is the mechanism that chooses. It subjects its awareness to only the limited drop of water, which has separated out from the wave into the sand. The left brain collapses the wave function; perceiving with limitations, to see exactly what it expects to see.

When we learn to expand our awareness into a state of playfulness, beyond any expectations, agendas, or attachment to outcomes, beyond what *we expect to see,* beyond thinking, then we enter into the domain of right brain awareness. By perceiving via the intuitive right brain, we are able to readily uncollapse the wave function into various possibility waves that await our further recognition.

The intuitive part of our brain, often referred to as the right brain, is a *parallel processor* that is able to track and follow multiple waves of possibilities simultaneously. The right brain can track patterns of information as probabilities *before* they become actualized. The language of the right brain is symbolic in nature and is very pattern oriented. It can track and follow connections that typically are not captured by the segregating serial processing of the left brain. The right brain appears to be governed by waves of interconnecting grids of possibilities. It is able to follow many waves *prior* to their becoming droplets of choice in the sand.

By dropping down into the field of the heart, we enter into a coherent state of awareness, thus bypassing the segregation and limitations of the mind and accessing the totality of consciousness before the wave collapses.

We go directly to the sea of coherent potential that resides in the field of the heart. We tap into consciousness potential by connecting to the most authentic part of ourselves that knows itself as whole, limitless, timeless, and dimensionless. We leverage coherence within a unified field when we drop into heart-centered awareness. There is no *doing* from that state of heart-centered being. It is an altered state of consciousness that, when embodied, becomes a vehicle for a new reality based in unity, love, and limitless potential.

Dropping into the torus field of the heart is as easy as breathing. We usually do not think about breathing, and yet it happens. Similarly, we often do not notice when we are in or out of our heart space. Noticing heart-centered awareness assists us in consistently and effortlessly accessing a space of grace where transformation is most likely to occur.

Practical Play: Dropping Down into the Field of the Heart

- Breathe in. On your exhale, simply relax your physiology. Drop your shoulders and allow your awareness to relax into the center of your being or your physical body. Notice the calmness and stillness and absence of thought. From this space, notice what you notice. What information begins to well up from your inner being?
- Ask an open-ended question, like, "What would I notice if I were to allow my awareness to move back into the heart field?" or "Where am I *in relation to* the field of my heart?" Follow that awareness and connect to it. From this space, notice what you notice.
- Consider that the field of the heart is what you are. The electromagnetic field of the heart is one of the first things that pops through the vacuum. Therefore, you are always in your heart. Awareness is what moves us in and out of resonance with the heart space.

- Imagine an elevator (E-love-ator). See a miniature version of yourself stepping into the elevator and allow for the doors to close. Press the Down button. Follow your awareness as the elevator descends out of your head, down through your throat, and even further down into your chest cavity. Allow for the elevator doors to open. Notice what you notice when you step out of the elevators into that space of no space and no place.
- Take a moment to feel into someone or something you love. Feel that connection. Notice the feeling and allow for that feeling to move through your entire body. Invite that feeling to center in the torsion field of your heart and then ask it to speak to you.
- Recognize that the field of the heart is connected to everything. Notice in your awareness that you are not separate—a separate body or being. See yourself as a vitamin C tablet. Like dropping an effervescent vitamin C tablet into a glass of water, drop yourself through your awareness and feel it within as your sense of separation dissolves. Notice that you feel a sense of dropping *in* and expanding *out* simultaneously. There is no separation between you and everything else. You are present in the here and now and also present everywhere. Ask your heart what it would tell you if you were to listen to it, now.
- Get silly! See a waterslide from your head to a pool in the field of the heart. Energetically pop your eyeballs out of your head, drop them onto the slide, and let them drop into the pool with a big splash. As your eyeballs resurface, notice your attention from the field of the heart.
- Notice the constant flow of thoughts in your brain or awareness without attachment to them. The more thoughts we have, the less likely we will be to listen to our heart. See your thoughts as clouds floating by. Do not attach to them. Observe them neutrally with a sense of curiosity and without judgment. Observing thoughts and experiences without judgment keeps us in a state of heart-centered awareness.
- Pay attention to genuine desires. Desires well up from the field of the heart and are cues or placeholders by which our awareness gets our attention. Desires *are*

the language of the heart speaking to us. When we listen, we move into a flow where desires become manifestations and experiences.

- Trust yourself. One way to notice, speak, and listen from the heart is to start trusting in yourself. The more you develop a sense of trust in yourself, the more your heart will lead in navigating your consciousness. The more you resonate in trust, the more your mind will follow your heart's intelligence.

- Let go of all sense of not being in your heart. Remember, the *thought of a problem* can become the problem. Ask yourself, "If I knew what I might notice were I to listen to my heart, regardless of what anyone else might suggest, what methods of dropping into my heart might I discover?"

It is useful to consider that the field of the heart is a space of no space, so it is not really something you drop into, per se. Rather, it is something you already are but have perhaps moved away from in awareness. Sometimes it is easier to see the heart field expanding around you like a pink bubble of unconditional love. Notice how expanded you feel when centered in this bubble.

While initially it is common not to sense or feel anything when we drop into the field of the heart, there often does tend to be a bubbling up or a wave of sheer joy emanating from this sea of potential. This state of joy heralds a return to our natural state of being as universal consciousness, and its infinite potential moves through us without resistance. Joy may be present regardless of external circumstances, and it is a powerfully graceful side effect of heart-centered awareness.

We can access our full potential when we move beyond the perspectives of what we think we know into the field of the heart. Any rigid adherence to ideas and beliefs about anything creates limiting parameters that shroud us from expanding into the realm of indeterminacy, where all things are possible.

By opening into not-knowing, we gain access to everything that spans beyond the inkling of what we may know.

From an expansive space of not-knowing, our awareness moves from a limited perspective into that which is perspective-less and limitless. Knowing nothing provides access to the all.

SIX

Two Points to Pointlessness

Truth is always the shortest distance between two points.
—*Sun Myung Moon*

The Two Point is an incredible construct that is unique to the original ME morphic field that was developed by Dr. Richard Bartlett. The construct has evolved to become a powerful exercise for eliciting, noticing, and experiencing change in all facets of reality.

The Two Point is a method of engaging in an ongoing conversation with universal consciousness. The method leverages awareness to expand beyond resonance with what we are currently noticing or experiencing so that we may witness the unfolding of something different. The Two Point allows us to connect *what is* with *what we desire to experience*. The Two Point is an ongoing dance with universal consciousness that enables us to easily move awareness from where we perceive ourselves to be and into the transformation we seek to embody as experience.

Originally, Dr. Bartlett developed the Two Point as a measurement tool to calibrate change on the physical body. A chiropractor and a naturopathic physician, he would locate a point on the physical body that seemed stuck, hard, or rigid and then choose another point that seemed equally stuck, hard, or rigid *or* less stuck, hard, or rigid. When he connected these two points in his awareness, he noticed that both points visibly and physically dissolved and then resolved into something different.

A discernible transformation transpired with the Two Point each time he used it. Pain patterns disappeared, bones realigned, and people felt different. But that was not all he noticed. Patterns completely unrelated to the two points he had chosen would change, too. Longstanding depression lifted, relationships improved, and finances increased. There appeared to be no limit to the types of changes that were occurring.

The amazing transformations that occurred from this simple awareness exercise sent Dr. Bartlett on a journey into the holographic nature of reality and quantum physics as he sought to explain these seemingly inexplicable outcomes.

Since the initial discovery of the Two Point more than a decade ago, our understanding of how it works and why it works has evolved significantly. We now understand that there is no real point to the Two Point. The point of the Two Point is to access *pointlessness.* Pointlessness is what the Two Point enables us to attain easily and effortlessly.

The Two Point enables our individual awareness to move from dual points of perspective into the all that is pointless, perspective-less, and distinction-less. The Two Point moves awareness beyond duality and into the unity that is universal consciousness and its infinite potentials.

Any explanation offers language as a means to articulate something that no words can adequately explain. Words as carrier waves convey what we perceive might be happening, but not what is *actually* happening. We can never, with absolute certainty, know what is actually happening. The moment we decide we are certain, we actually limit what we can access. Thus, all explanations are simply bridges that allow our individual awareness to comprehend something that is beyond explanation. Remember, concepts and explanations are maps that describe the territory of consciousness, but they are not the territory itself.

From a quantum-physics perspective, the Two Point allows us to *uncollapse* the wave function, to move from our current configuration of conscious expression and access different possibility states that are available but which we are not yet in resonance with. When we consciously engage and follow a Two Point, we are able to perform a weak *collapse of the wave function,* which occurs when we notice what is different, not what is the same. This allows our awareness to move into rapport with changes that have already begun to unfold.

The changes or transformations that become available to us following a Two Point are like ripples in a pond when we drop a pebble into it. The ripples or waves reverberate outward indefinitely to all the patterns that comprise an individual's holographic experience of reality. There are no limits to the changes we can experience when engaging with a Two Point.

The Two Point allows us to move our perspective from fixed, immutable, particle-based realities into fluid, flowing, wave-based possibilities that are ever present and available to us when we notice them. The Two Point bridges Newtonian forces, epitomized by the mechanistic physics of separatism, with holographic resonance and the quantum nature of entanglement.

All patterns in reality are connected and, therefore, all patterns that comprise an individual's experience of reality are subject to change. Yes, all patterns can change.

The Two Point connects the part of us that perceives itself as separate—physical, discrete, and stuck in expressions as patterns—to that which is the all and which appears to be flexible, malleable, and unlimited in possibility. The Two Point connects us with consciousness potential.

From a simple mathematical perspective, the Two Point connects us to infinity, as well as to zero. Consider this: If we place two points on a piece of paper and then connect them, we form a line. If we divide the line and continue to further divide the line, there will never be a point in space where we cannot continue dividing the line. By unifying the initially divided two points, we see that infinite divisions or infinite expressions can stem from the initial connection. There are limitless potential distinctions that can occur. The Two Point puts us in direct resonance with the infinite and allows for limitless consciousness potential to unfold in limitless expressions of change.

The Two Point also allows our awareness of three-dimensional reality to move into a zero-point reality that has access to the all. When we connect the two points together in our awareness, we dissolve the dual perspective maintained from each discrete point, expanding awareness into no-point, zero dimension, or dimensionlessness. We are launched in our awareness to a level of consciousness that, through unity, transcends duality and moves freely among the binding polarities that are expressed within a dimensional experience.

The Two Point enables us to observe reality from beyond duality while still embracing duality. It provides us with a method for effectively navigating the realms of distinction and contrast that are the hallmarks of three-dimensional reality.

The Two Point is also a beacon for creating resonance with established morphic fields, such as ME. It connects us with a morphic field and allows for the field to engage with us to reconfigure our personal and collective consciousness. The Two Point creates a portal for that which is grace and pure potential to begin singing its lyrics of possibilities to us and through us.

While the Two Point may at first be something you choose to do, it soon evolves into something that you become. The Two Point becomes a natural extension of awareness that expands our limited perspective to one of unlimited potential. It is an ongoing, eternal, and intimate dialog between individual and universal consciousness. The Two Point carries us from what we are noticing and experiencing right now to noticing and experiencing that anything is possible.

There is no point to the Two Point, and its pointlessness means that there are no limitations to what can unfold for us. Notice what you notice, and while noticing, also notice what is different, not what is the same.

As the morphic field of ME has grown progressively stronger, we have noticed that it has become easier for students to recognize that the Two Point can be applied to anything and everything, as everything is consciousness.

Suggestions for Facilitating Awareness of Change with the Two Point

There truly is no correct or incorrect way to do the Two Point. There are, however, many useful suggestions and a few guiding principles for facilitating awareness of change. As we learned in an earlier chapter, martial artist Bruce Lee's tenets have been adapted into the field. To recap:

- Absorb what is useful.
- Discard the classical mess.
- No way as way.

In addition, the following corollaries are useful: drop down, place intent, and let go.

Drop down

Drop down into the field of the heart (see Chapter 5 for suggestions on how to do this easily and instantly). Drop down out of limiting thoughts into the space of nothing, into the field of the heart, where all is neutral and accessible as undifferentiated consciousness potential.

Place intent

When initially engaging with the Two Point, our intention is simply to notice what we notice, and then notice what is different. Our intention is to pick any two points that capture our attention. Where awareness goes, information flows. Again, where awareness goes, information flows. The two points can be anywhere. At first, it will be easiest for some to notice two points on the body and to actually touch them.

For example, I might notice that my attention initially is drawn to my right hip, and that can be my first point in the Two Point. To facilitate noticing, I place my right hand on my hip. I then notice somewhere else that draws my attention, such as my left knee, and that would represent my second point. I then place my left hand there to further facilitate my awareness of it.

Wherever your attention goes as you choose two points, trust it. Simply pick one point. Pick a second point. The points may be where you notice pain or constriction, or they may be points that simply catch your attention for no apparent reason whatsoever.

Touching the two points is not necessary to engage in a Two Point. However, touching can be helpful when learning how to notice change following the Two Point. Tactile interaction enables the multiple sensory receptors in our hands to gather information, which facilitates our ability to notice, sense, and perceive even more information than if we relied only on other forms of awareness. Touching with hands can be extremely useful when beginning to play in the field. However, awareness of two points can occur with or without the experience of touch.

Now, simply connect the two points in your awareness, as if they are no longer two separate points but actually are merged as one, indistinct connection.

Sometimes, it helps to envision yourself as a child drawing or playing Connect the Dots.

If drawing, see each point as two separate dots on a piece of paper and then merge the dots with a curvy line, as if you are creating a smiley face. After all, the shortest distance to unity is a smile!

If playing Connect the Dots, connect the two points with a line. Notice that the two points are no longer separate, but instead, are part of a greater continuum or whole. The two points, initially particles of immutable distinction, have merged into a wave of potential through our awareness.

Let go

This is perhaps one of the most important suggestions for engaging with the Two Point as a conduit for the field. What does it mean to let go? It means to let go of observing the connection made through the two points. Let go of looking to see if something has happened. Let go of focusing on what is or is not happening.

How do you let go? Simply look away. Shift your awareness to something elsewhere, such as a movie you really like. See yourself walking barefoot on a beach. Play with a puppy dog. My favorite way to let go is to go stress-free shoe-shopping in my mind.

Let go can also mean dropping back down into the heart. Letting go is not a literal letting go of touching the two points, although it can be. It is easier to let go through awareness than physically with the hands. Really, the hands have nothing to do with what is or is not happening.

Let go means to stop observing a state of *no-change* so that consciousness and its infinite potential can express through you as something different.

Let go means to get out of the way so that the field of consciousness potential can express through you.

Let go also means to let go of any and all expectations relative to what the outcome or result may look like. Let go of the lust for results, and results will show up in ways you cannot possibly imagine in advance. When we are focused on results, we are attached to an outcome. When we are attached to an outcome, our very limited focus on a specific, predefined change *and* its polarity of *no-change* limits the options that may be available to us. Attachment to an outcome with a lust for results also keeps our awareness resonating in the gap between what we are experiencing and the desired result.

Notice what is different, not what is the same, and observe as changes unfold. Some people notice immediate shifts in their sense of themselves. They often notice a feeling of expansion, a peaceful feeling, a wobbly feeling, a shift in balance, a change in breathing patterns, less pain or no pain at all, more mobility and range of motion, spontaneous movements, freedom from stress, more clarity, a sense of connection, and laughter and/or joy for no apparent reason.

Whatever we notice, it is part of how the field is moving through us and reconfiguring the various patterns of information that are resonating in our own field, some of which are constricting our access to flow.

It is common *not* to know exactly what is different. It is common *not* to be able to precisely describe a difference. It is normal and truly okay to not notice what is different in the immediate moment. However, when something different shows up in your awareness a little while later, pay attention.

Whatever occurs for you is exactly what is useful in the moment. Even being uncertain about what has happened can be useful, for uncertainty is a space where patterns can freely reconfigure into different expressions.

Be conscious that changes will continue to ripple through your personal awareness and experiences after the interaction of the Two Point appears to have completed itself. The continuous evolution of your awareness is *never* done but is instead an ever-present unfolding from potentiality *to* possibility *to* actualization as realized experience. Continue to pay attention to whatever shows up that is different in your ever-expanding personal awareness.

The more we notice what is *different* versus *what is the same*, the more we establish resonance with the unfolding of consciousness potential expressing itself through change and transformation.

Practical Play with the Two Point

The Two Point is an ongoing conversation with universal consciousness. This means that the Two Point enables us to move our awareness from what appears to be happening now, in a fixed manner, into the flow of multiple possibilities. Allow the first point to be the limitless potential of the field of the heart and the second point to be whatever captures your attention. Where awareness goes, information flows. Notice what you notice, as you flow into something different.

The two-point can also be described as follows:

First point: Where attention and awareness is presently configured. "Notice what I notice" and "What am I noticing now?"

Second point: Where attention goes in terms of "What have I yet to notice that is different?"

The connection between the two points of reference allows us to establish resonance with a different configuration and experience an ease of unfolding into becoming the change we desire to experience. The Two Point is a construct for perspective that allows us to access that which is without perspective and distinction — the all —

and to gently choose a different potentiality to actualize through observation. Choose.

Even if you do not get the Two Point as a concept, the process is easily accessible through the morphic field of ME, which facilitates it to support and sustain change. Initially, I did not get the Two Point. I did not see the point of identifying two points on my body, or any-where else for that matter, to effect change. I thought it was silly. Yet, despite what I thought, or understood, or did not understand, I was curious. Curiosity about the Two Point is sufficient for engaging in the process. When I did my first Two Point on myself, I did not know what I was doing. So I just followed the mantra: drop down, place intent, and let go.

I dropped down into my heart. From there, I placed intent and chose two points, without thinking or hesita-tion. I chose my left hip and my neck, simply because they caught my attention. I chose those two points because I could. I was tempted to hesitate, but I realized that hesitation was not trust. So, I trusted and chose those two points, both of which seemed random. I touched them. When I connected the two points in my awareness, like a smiley face, I felt myself sort of melt into the couch as if my body was no longer separate from the furniture. That was the first thing I noticed that was different.

Next, I noticed that I felt lighter and more peaceful. Then, to my surprise, I noticed that the pain in my left foot, which had bothered me for several weeks, had lessened significantly. The following day, the foot pain was totally gone.

I was amazed. I'd had no idea what I was doing. All I thought I was doing was choosing two points, letting go, and noticing what was different. I didn't try to get rid of pain. I was simply noticing two points on my body as a connection. In that connection, the particles of experience transformed to a wave of potential. In that potential, my experience of myself, along with my pain, changed. Hooray!

I considered my first Two Point a fluke, but I certainly was amazed that my foot pain had dissipated. Perhaps it was a coincidence that the pain went away after the Two Point. Even so, it was a meaningful coincidence because the pattern was really different.

So I tried the Two Point again, and again I did not have any intention other than to drop down, place intent, and let go. This time I chose one point on my body, my left shoulder, and a second point off my body, approximately three feet in front of me. I felt myself sway and wobble. I thought that was weird.

I asked, "How is this useful?" Immediately, I noticed that my irritation about a work issue was less pronounced. I also noticed that I felt happier and more connected to my family. I felt more present and motivated to finish a project that I had been postponing for awhile.

Over the next several days, I noticed what else was different. I slept soundly after months of interrupted slumber. I woke up naturally, on time, without my alarm clock, which was quite different for me. All were welcome changes. The more I noticed what was different, the more differences I experienced. The Two Point had significantly facilitated my ability not only to experience change, but also to notice it.

Nowadays, I leverage the construct of the Two Point with focused intention in all that I do. I drop down into the field of my heart and consider where I would like to establish resonance. I can pay attention to the desire to experience something in my life and consider that desire to be the first point. The second point of the Two Point enables me to connect to the information in the corresponding field of information that will facilitate that desire. For example, if I want to learn how to speak a foreign language, then connecting to the morphic field of that specific language through the Two Point will allow ease and flow into that learning experience to facilitate it, by virtue of the established connection. With the Two Point, rather than try to master a field as if it were something separate from us, we can become one with it.

I often play with the Two Point as a matter of practice, because developing this skill when it apparently doesn't matter means it is easily available when it does matter. Sometimes, I Two Point a slow-moving line in the grocery store into a state of flow. Or, although I might intend to speed up the line, in the process of the Two Point I notice that, suddenly, I don't care how slow it is because, for example, the person behind me has initiated an interesting dialog. The Two Point can help us shift our state so that everything around us appears to shift, too.

My favorite time to do a Two Point is at the start of each day. I drop down into the field of my heart, and this becomes my first point. I choose a second point anywhere I want to represent the completion of my perfect day. I do not decide in advance what a "perfect day" needs to be like, or look like, or what exactly needs to occur in that perfection. I simply trust from the field of the heart and connect to the resonant vibration of what feels perfect, that which is optimal to me in that moment.

I then let go into my day, knowing the choice is already done. In fact, it is done before it has begun. I simply need to pay attention and notice all the cues that universal consciousness provides to confirm what has already been created through resonance via the Two Point.

It is useful to remember that the Two Point is a conversation with consciousness in which we notice what we notice now, and then, we notice something different in the very next moment. In the same manner that universal consciousness has infinite potential and infinite expressions, there are infinite ways to engage with a Two Point and to notice the Two Point as a facilitator for change. The Two Point is also a process to combine heart-centered awareness with focused intent. However you choose to notice and experience the Two Point for yourself is perfect. Invite your awareness to continue expanding so that can see that everything in your reality can be experienced through an ongoing series of Two Points, connecting you with all.

SEVEN

Time Travel through the Eternal Now

The only reason for time is so that everything doesn't happen at once.

—Albert Einstein

We are still here and now. Don't worry. This chapter isn't about literally going back to the future in a Lamborghini or forward to the past like a *Star Trek* episode. Practically speaking, the application of Time Travel is an effective strategy for expanding our resonance with limitless potential to manifest as experience.

In ME seminars, we thoroughly explain the physics of Time Travel. Because this is not a book on physics, we will not focus extensively on the theories. However, as before, I will reference some basic principles in quantum physics and torsion-field physics as metaphorical constructs that will show you how to apply Time Travel to your everyday experiences. Although the constructs may not be absolutely true, and all are subject to interpretation, what is important is that all of them are potentially useful.

What Is Time?

The dictionary defines time as "a nonspatial continuum in which events occur in apparently irreversible succession from the past through the present to the future."

Hmmm? *Apparently* irreversible succession? Perhaps this means that we don't really know with any absolute degree of certainty what time is. What's the story about time in quantum physics? Well, it depends on whom we ask and which theory is percolating at the moment. Physicists are all over the place with respect to time.

Many theories attempt to build upon the limitations of previous theories. Bear in mind that all the theories are based on initially incomplete and possibly false premises. Perhaps none of the theories are ultimately accurate. Maybe they are all just close approximations. It's a bit like the time on our wristwatches. If we all watched them together, we would discover that they are not totally synchronized, and some are more accurate than others. As they say, even the broken watches are correct twice a day! Nonetheless, a general idea of what time might be helps us organize our awareness and track our experiences. Physics is the same way in terms of pointing a hand in the right direction.

Time as We Perceive It

Typically, we experience time as linear and unidirectional. We notice our lives through a series of experiences that are marked in our awareness by a *seemingly* forward progression of time. What *apparently* happened yesterday is considered the past. What *may* happen tomorrow is considered the future, and what *appears* to be happening now is considered the present moment. We have been led to believe that we cannot change the past because it is already gone, and some think we cannot impact the future because it is not yet here. Supposedly, all we can truly do is to live in the moment. Live in the *now*. Really? Live in the *now?* Interesting enough, by the time we observe the present moment, it *is* the past and we are already in the future. However, we miss the future as the current *now* because we are busy noticing the past, which used to be the present. When we really consider time, it's a fascinating quandary.

To better understand the nature of time, we could explore various theories of quantum physics. Many theories seem contradictory or involve so much math that they are unintelligible even to some physicists. Overall, the consensus about the true nature of time, at this time, is that we do not fully know or understand it. There is a general premise that the arrow of time only moves forward.

Regarding this premise, physicist A. Z. Jones has noted that,

> while this is certainly true, the curious thing is that the laws of physics are time reversible, which is to say that the laws themselves look as if they would work perfectly well if the universe played out in reverse. From a physics standpoint, there's no real reason why the arrow of time should by necessity be moving forward.[1]

A very applicable piece of information is the transactional interpretation of quantum mechanics (TIQM), proposed in 1986 by John G. Cramer at the University of Washington, which explores quantum interactions of time as follows: There is a standing wave that travels forward in time, referred to as a *retarded wave*, and also a standing wave that travels backward in time, referred to as an *advanced wave*. Where the waves intersect, a cancellation occurs, creating the present moment. Cramer claimed that there was no observer effect or collapse of the wave function, at all, but rather that time is an ongoing flow of intersecting standing waves. This work implies that time is bidirectional, not unidirectional. Cramer also did some pilot research with photons, demonstrating that photons could travel backward and forward in time.[2] Remember, we are made of photons!

Further research into the holographic universe theory provided even more puzzling pieces to the mystery of time. American author Michael Talbot elaborates on theoretical physicist David Bohm's theory of time in *The Holographic Universe*:

> In a holographic universe, even time and space could no longer be viewed as fundamentals. Because concepts such

as location break down in a universe in which nothing is truly separate from anything else, time and three-dimensional space would also have to be viewed as projections of this deeper order. At its deeper level reality is a sort of superhologram in which the past, present, and future all exist simultaneously. This suggests that given the proper tools it might even be possible to someday reach into the superholographic level of reality and pluck out scenes from the long-forgotten past.[3]

David Bohm is not the only researcher who found evidence that the universe is a hologram. Working independently in the field of brain research, Stanford neurophysiologist Karl Pribram also explored holographic theory relative to the mind. He concluded that memories are not stored in the mind. Rather, they are stored in a hologram.

Expanding upon principles of holographic resonance, combined with some compelling principles in quantum physics to enhance practical application, consider the possibility that every experience we have had is encoded holographically in our personal fields via intersecting standing waves that form nodal points.

What Is a Nodal Point?

A nodal point is a standing wave pattern. What is a standing wave pattern? Why is it standing, and whom is it waving at?

According to physicists,

the wave pattern associated with the natural frequencies of an object is characterized by points that appear to be standing still. For this reason, the pattern is often called a "standing wave pattern." The points in the pattern that are standing still are referred to as nodal points or nodal positions. These positions occur as the result of the destructive interference of incident and reflected waves.[4]

The body, as a hologram, has access to these nodal points at all times, whether the mind is conscious of them or not.

Simply speaking, *if* time were linear and mapped like a road, then nodal points of experience would be represented by the equivalent of speed bumps. Every nodal point has an address in the hologram. Encoded in each nodal point is information specific to an experience. It is not a memory per se. It is information locked in a specific configuration of consciousness expressed as a holographic nodal point. The nodal point itself may have a charge, but the encoded information is neutral.

Our continual resonance with information locked in nodal points that were encoded in the *past* keeps us seemingly stuck in perpetuating a pattern in the *present*. In other words, this may be why stuff doesn't seem to change. Consider that almost all of our problems or patterns were not created *right now*. To change a pattern from the past in the *now*, we can leverage Time Travel to access the nodal point that is storing the information that we want to address, and open, and then release to reconfigure consciousness potential.

As a result, any experience encoded in the past can be resonantly imprinted for a different potentiality and can transform into something different. It is not only that our perception around any given experience may change, but also that we may find that we no longer even resonate with the experience. Sometimes, it is as though it didn't even happen, at all.

Remember, change the resonance of the encoded information, and you can change the experience.

While it may seem somewhat nonsensical to our logical minds, playing with Time Travel is one of the most powerful ways to change our experience in the now, because most of the perceived now is a result of past resonance. Just because our logical, linear minds consider this a nonsensical notion, does not mean it is not true or possible. That it does not make sense may be because time, as we have come to know it, is geared toward linearity and forward direction. Our linear minds have been entrained to perceive the concept of time, through our awareness, as moving only in one direction.

Our rational minds, as logical linear processors, can observe only limited, successive sequences of events. Time is how consciousness keeps track of its movement. Similarly, if we wish to organize how a series of events might have happened or may happen, we leverage time as a marker for our awareness. For instance, each time something happens, the event creates a holographic nodal point in our personal field.

It occurs to me that time being nonlinear makes total sense to the intuitive brain, which is a parallel processor. The field of the heart also knows that linear time is merely one way that consciousness may observe itself as a construct that appears to travel from one moment to another. However, the dance of time is more accurately concentric or torsion-like in nature, and not actually linear, at all. The eternal now is forever in a tango with all possibilities simultaneously.

Time as Torsion and Torsion-Field Physics

Time is more closely an approximation of ongoing enfoldment and an expression of torsion fields. Consciousness *is* spinning. Perhaps this is how our individual awareness engages with torsion fields to create our perpetual experiences of time.

In 1913, Dr. Eli Cartan was the first to demonstrate clearly that the flow of space and time in Einstein's general theory of relativity not only curves, but also possesses a spinning or spiraling movement within itself, which is known as torsion.[5] It is generally accepted that the space surrounding the Earth, and perhaps the entire galaxy, has what is called right-handed spin, which simply means that energy is influenced to spin clockwise as it travels through a physical vacuum. This torsion research was expanded by the work of Kozyrev in Russia. Using rotation and vibration in laboratory experiments, systematic research was able to demon-strate that torsion fields influence the flow of time.[6]

Now, let's bring it back to ourselves. How does un-derstanding that time is torsion affect us?

Heart Field as a Vehicle for Time Travel

As we learned in Chapter 5, the field of the heart is a torsion field. When we drop into the center of the field of the heart, we access the part of us that is limitless, distinctionless, and also timeless.

In my experience, the vortex of the field of the heart exists outside the continuum of space-time. It is a hyperdimensional, time-travel device, allowing access to all information, all-inclusively, and simultaneously. It also occurs to me that, as awareness moves distally from the vortex toward the outer rings of the torsion fields, we become more subject to linear space-time and the persistent, albeit illusory, law of cause and effect.

When we are in the field of the heart, we are in the flow and void of resistance. We are in a space of grace, where anything can happen, and where nothing takes time because everything is available to us instantly through the eternal-now. Consider the experience of being totally engaged in a creative process or immersed in an endeavor that enraptures your awareness so much that you *lose all track of time*. In terms of perceived linear time, hours may go by, and yet it feels like only a minute has passed. Or consider the experience of meeting someone for the first time and connecting so totally heart-to-heart that it feels like you have known them for years, or all your life, or even forever, when in fact, in linear time, you have known them for only a few mo-ments.

Torsion Fields as Containers for Information

As I've previously shared, every experience we have ever had is encoded in nodal points. These nodal points are, essentially, torsion fields of information. The individual torsion fields of experience are contained holographically within our personal fields and remain forever connected to the unified torsion field of the heart. Re-encoding prior experiences holographically via torsion fields of information is accessible to all of us who choose to playfully leverage the construct of Time Travel. While our minds access the information along the continuum of linear time, our hearts can follow these interconnected holographic torsion fields at all times.

Practical Play: Anyone, Anywhere, Anytime

Dropping down into the field of the heart, while also availing ourselves of linear time so that our minds can follow along in a familiar way, gives us access to various torsion fields of information that are encoded as nodal points of experience in our individual fields. These nodal points of experience are often in resonance with, and powered by, much larger morphic fields.

Through the act of observation, which entangles the observer with the observed, we are able to release nodal points of information encoded therein and return them back to pure potential to await further recognition as something different. Time Travel is an awesome way to change our resonance with past experiences or even establish resonance with a *future potential* to expedite the manifestation process.

While engaging in Time Travel may feel linear, initially, it is not linear, at all. The act of counting to observe time is not what creates a transformation. The change or transformation occurs as we identify the nodal point or torsion field of encoded information, while the act of counting is a construct for knowing where we are as we navigate through the field of consciousness potential.

Play is a key to Time Travel. Time Travel is not about being right or fixing stuff; rather, it is simply about dropping down into the field of the heart and being curious.

- Drop down: Drop down into the field of the heart.
- Place intent: You can begin with the Two Point. Choose any two points on or off the body that get your attention. The points can be meaningless and appear random, or you can choose a point in awareness that represent a pattern you are experiencing and a point that represents the desired change.
- Following the two-point connection, think or state out loud your present age or the present age of the person you are playing with. This establishes a zero-point reference for time. It is akin to Dorothy clicking her heels three times and saying, "There's no place like home, there's no place like home," and finding herself home. Home is where the heart is, and stating your present age while dropping into the heart is a useful reference point from which to begin navigating through the limitless playground of consciousness potential.
- Beginning with the present age you stated, count backwards in increments of one to five years until you sense, perceive, notice, or feel a shift, either in yourself or with the person you have selected to play with.
- Let go: Let go of attachment to what the change is supposed to be and to any assumptions around it.
- Notice: Notice what is different instead of noticing what is the same. Anything you notice is useful. Change is change is change.

Time Travel for Transformation

You can use Time Travel to play with specific issues. For example, recently I had taken a long run in too short a time and, as a result, was noticing and experiencing pain in my left knee. Or so I thought. To change up the pattern, I thought I would play with Time Travel. So, I dropped down into the field of my heart and chose two points. The first point was the knee that was not in pain, simply because that is where my awareness landed. The second point was my right ear. I did not physically touch either point. Rather I held them in my awareness and noticed a connection.

Then, starting with my present age, I began to count backwards in increments of five years because that was what occurred to me. Even though the perceived injury had happened only days ago, my curiosity was drawn to count in increments of five years. Well, when I landed on an age twenty-five years ago, I heard a loud pop in my injured knee. Then, I noticed what I noticed. The pain was gone. I also noticed a flash of memories from an event that had happened, lo and behold, precisely twenty-five years in the past.

If I had tried to "fix" my injured knee by deliberately time-traveling back to a few days before the injury, it may or may or may not have made a difference. However, by letting go of the need to fix anything and simply playing with Time Travel, I was able to release a nodal point of information that had encoded many years ago, which also released a new pattern of painful expression contained within my knee.

Time Travel for Releasing Stagnant Thoughts and Emotions

While Time Travel is a great method for transforming physical conditions, I love Time Travel as a process for releasing old, stagnant thoughts and emotions. Much of how we react in the moment is a response to some experience we have encoded in the past. Thus, when we are entangled in an emotive charge that originated in the past, we are not freely responding to what is occurring now. Time Travel is a great method for releasing stuck

114

notions or emotions that may be preventing us from responding to the moment clearly, freely, and in flow.

Recently, I was in a conversation with an authoritative figure who I felt was not listening to me. I was offering my perspective, and rather than acknowledging what I had conveyed, the person repeatedly interrupted me, contradicted me, and proceeded to argue with me, only to conclude exactly what I had initially shared as though it was their own original idea. I found myself growing increasingly angry; I felt totally disrespected, not heard, and not valued. The experience brought up all the emotions that I had ever felt in similar experiences in the past.

I almost let this person have a piece of my mind, with expletives, and then I had the peace of mind to drop into my heart and play with Time Travel. In less than a minute, I had traversed through consciousness, navigating back five, ten, fifteen, . . . twenty years ago. Twenty years in the past, I noticed what felt like a ball of yarn stuck in my throat, and then it cleared almost instantly. So did my anger and frustration and discontent. I felt like laughing. The person in front of me had triggered me into a state of feeling completely disempowered that apparently had its origins more than two decades ago. Although I could not remember what happened in the past at the age I had traveled to, it does not matter. What matters is what is noticeably different. Following the play with Time Travel, I experienced an instant return to my center of well-being. I was neutral. I was calm and clear. I felt happy.

From this powerful state, I was able to articulate to the seemingly rude person that, if they were interested in my support and insight, I was eager and willing to provide it. However, I would not participate in the conversation unless we had complete agreement to listen, not interrupt, and to acknowledge the information shared in a non-confrontational manner.

To my surprise, I received a very favorable response, filled with the very respect that I was showing for myself in this engagement. I had time-traveled myself into a worthy experience that was precisely the present that I desired.

For Optimal Results, Let Go of Any Agenda

Optimal play with Time Travel occurs when you let go of any agenda, in other words, it is not useful to try to specifically fix something by specifically traversing to the moment before you think something occurred. We never know the exact inception of the pattern and thus, being flexible with Time Travel is the most useful way to play with the process and notice change. Time Travel works by releasing the resonance of a pattern. The exact moment that an injury occurs or emotional pain surfaces may not be where the torsion field of information is stored holographically, or where the pattern is encoded nodally along the continuum of time.

In fact, pattern inception may occur years prior to an experience. Releasing the resonance where the nodal point occurs naturally, rather than where you decide it *should be* or *might be,* allows you to leverage Time Travel to realize more beneficial outcomes. Remember, releasing resonance or information at a nodal point requires that you not decide on an age (or reference point in time) in advance. Instead, get out of the way and allow the field to work through you. As you embrace the flexibility of consciousness accessible through Time Travel, you gain greater access to consistent transformations.

Time Travel into the Future Expedites Manifestation

Time Travel into the future is an awesome method for expediting the manifestation process. By traversing into the future and connecting with a nodal point of information potential, we establish resonance with a future version of ourselves that is already having an experience. This increases the likelihood that the experience will occur. Time-traveling into the future is a super-fun, super-easy method to access a version of ourselves that is seasoned in an experience we have not yet had. Traveling into the future enables us to gather information from a future version of ourselves that perhaps has the benefit of hindsight and wisdom from experiences already completed. Travel forward to meet the accomplished part of yourself and ask how you did it so easily. The method for traveling forward in time is the same as the method for traveling back in time. Remember, time is not unidirectional. Thus, we are able to traverse in both directions freely with flexibility.

Essentially, when we travel into the past or the future and observe a pattern differently, it is as if that experience as initially encoded in our field did not occur in exactly the same way. The perceived experience will be different, implying a different experiential outcome, as though it had happened in a different universe.

EIGHT

Parallel Universes
Portals of Oscillating Possibilities

If I had a world of my own, everything would be nonsense.
Nothing would be what it is, because everything would be
what it isn't. And contrary wise, what is, it wouldn't be.
And what it wouldn't be, it would. You see?
                    —*Lewis Carroll,* Alice in Wonderland

You may be surprised to hear that there is support for parallel universes from physicists. Mathematician and quantum theorist Hugh Everett III developed a parallel universes theory known as the many worlds interpretation (MWI). MWI is a quantum physics model that seeks to explain what happens outside the collapse of the wave function. The theory postulates that an actual wave function collapse may never actually fully occur. The theory states that there is a universal wave function and that every possibility that can occur *does* occur. All possibilities become actualities, albeit in alternate realities.[1]

> The many worlds interpretation was created by Hugh Everett III in 1956 in his doctoral thesis, The Theory of the Universal Wave Function. It was later popularized by the efforts of physicist Bryce DeWitt.... The Everett postulate implies that the entire universe (being a single isolated system) continuously exists in a superposition of multiple states. There is no point where the wave-function ever collapses within the universe, because that would imply that some portion of the universe doesn't follow the Schroedinger wavefunction.[2]

Universal Wave Function: Cloudy to Clarity

There are infinite possibilities that represent a coherent field of potential. The term *coherent* refers to a unified field of potentials that have not yet expressed into distinctions or experiences. Imagine looking up at the sky and seeing only one consolidated cloud spread across the horizon. In fact, imagine that all you see is cloud and there is no sign of anything else in the sky other than that single cloud that extends everywhere. This is a good description of a coherent field, as there are no distinctions in the unified cloud and nowhere is there evidence of clouds branching off from this singular cloud to assume separate shapes or formations.

Now, imagine that you perceive movement within the cloud and some clouds appear to have broken off from the unified cloud. Then, you would be observing clouds *decohering* from the undifferentiated, coherent field of cloud to form distinct cloud formations. If coherence is connection, then decoherence is the separation from indistinct to distinct expression.

Practical Play: Partly Cloudy to Sunny Skies

Practically speaking, here is how this pertains to us. Suppose you intend to take a vacation. The possibilities are infinite; you can go anywhere in the world.

Out of all places you might choose to travel, you research Bali, Hawaii, and the Bahamas as possible destinations. From the infinite field of vacation potentials, you are now considering three distinct options that have *decohered* into possibility states. They are possibility states because choice has not yet occurred. The next choices are dates and airlines. You may depart on February 18 or February 21 on either Sunshine Airlines or Ocean Airlines. With these travel options, you have several additional possibility states that have further *decohered* from the original three possibility states (Bali, Hawaii, and the Bahamas).

Let's say you decide to travel to Bali, departing February 18 on Sunshine Airlines. You have made a choice. You embark on this flight to this destination on this date and on this airline. You are aware, as an observer, that this is the choice you are experiencing as your reality. In quantum physics, according to the traditional collapse of the wave function theory, your subjective choice to go to Bali is affirmed by your observation and your experience. There is a single unfolding of reality.

Alternatively, according to MWI theory, something altogether different may be occurring. MWI theory views reality as an ever-branching, everlasting weave, where every possible outcome is realized. However, we do not notice these multibranched, alternative options for reality because they are happening in parallel or alternative universes.

So, according to MWI theory, while you chose to travel to Bali on February 18 on Sunshine Air, in an alternate or parallel universe, you also traveled to Hawaii and the Bahamas on both February 18 and February 21, on both Sunshine Air and Ocean Air. You did not notice these alternate or parallel universes because you were resonating in the Bali-verse, swimming with dolphins and lounging on the sand. Your conscious awareness as an observer is focused in Bali, and so that is all you notice and subsequently experience.

So, practically speaking, how is MWI or parallel universe theory useful? Remember, reality is a result of resonance with patterns of information. Where we resonate creates the template for our experiences. Parallel Universes, as an application, is a useful method for expanding our references and resonance with other aspects of ourselves. Because of this expansion, we are able to experience ourselves differently; we are able to easily and consistently tap into multiple options, which are extensions of consciousness that enable us to actually experience ourselves as the multifaceted, limitless beings that we truly are.

Desire Is the Fire

Pay close attention to desires that are inspired through the field of the heart. These are the inner sensations of curiosity that propel us toward taking action in a certain direction. Curiosity is not an impetus of thought that has been calculated through logic. Rather, heart-centered desire is the fire of the soul's yearning to express itself through form and experience. A creative impulse is sparked by the authentic desires that well up from the field of the heart; when listened to, these authentic desires lead us to experience the unfolding of our true magnificence.

For example, imagine you have a heart-felt desire to weave baskets underwater. You know it is a heart-felt desire because you can feel it in the core of your being. You have no experience with weaving baskets under water, and yet, a knowingness arises and the desired experience has a familiarity to it, even though you have not had the experience *as* an actual experience. This is a cue for you that an aspect of your awareness, or a part of your expanded, limitless self, is already adept at weaving baskets under water, albeit in a parallel universe. You simply need to align your awareness to resonate with that parallel universe and then pay attention to the cues that unfold from universal consciousness, which will lead you directly into that experience. Establishing resonance allows your awareness to align with desired outcomes without attaching to any specific outcome.

Note that applying the Parallel Universes method does not obviate the need to take action toward any intended goal. However, simply by virtue of establishing resonance with the part of your unlimited consciousness that is already having an experience in an alternate universe, you connect with that potential; this increases the likelihood, or probability that what will unfold in your awareness in this universe will match that parallel-universe experience.

It is useful to consider that how we appear to ourselves in the present moment is akin to what results from the collapse of the wave function. Out of all the possibilities available to us as limitless consciousness potential, we do not see ourselves objectively, as such; instead, we see ourselves subjectively, based on what we expect to see. Applying the Parallel Universes method allows us to expand our awareness so as to access multiple aspects of ourselves that we might not otherwise recognize. In addition, using Parallel Universes as a method allows us to reclaim aspects of ourselves that we may have negated or jettisoned previously. Through Parallel Universes, we can establish resonance with greater versions of ourselves.

Suppose that a mother of five children gave up her lifelong dream to become a professional opera singer so she could attend to the needs of her family. According to the MWI interpretation, in a parallel universe she *is* a professional opera singer. Thus, she can tap into that experience through establishing resonance with a parallel universe to expand her consciousness of what may still be possible now or, alternatively, to help mitigate the perceived loss of an option not chosen.

Resonance with What Has Already Been Done

Working with Parallel Universes is an awesome way to learn new skills. If you have a desire in your heart to grow into something more, that is the universe collaborating to inspire you to notice it. Applying Parallel Universes is an incredibly easy way to establish resonance with having already mapped, already learned, and already done the experience.

In addition, Parallel Universes is an extremely useful method for transforming longstanding conditions and patterns that are habitual ways of noticing and experiencing reality. For instance, in this universe, you may have chronic insomnia. In a parallel universe—or maybe several universes over in the *sleep* universe—is a version of you that sleeps soundly through the night. By establishing resonance with the version of you in a different universe, you can experience sleep in a different way here in this universe. The part of you that is already still sleeping is beckoning you to wake up to this possibility for yourself.

Practical Play: Integrating Use of Time Travel and Parallel Universes

Making use of Time travel and Parallel Universes may still mystify you. Are they theoretical, virtual, or actual? Whatever they may be, their practical applications for expanding our individual consciousness experiences are absolutely limitless.

The following is a somewhat linear, two-dimensional construct for playing with and understanding Parallel Universes. Although Time Travel and Parallel Universes may differ, we can use them together quite effectively.

Consider a Cartesian coordinate system that makes use of graphs to plot coordinates on x and y axes. The $(0,0)$ point on the x-y axes, or the zero coordinate point, represents us in our present resonance, that is, where we are right now in our current configuration of consciousness. In this construct, the x axis would represent Time Travel, providing us with flexibility of consciousness moving horizontally in time. The y axis would represent parallel universes, providing us with flexibility of consciousness moving vertically across universes. We can traverse universes in the present moment or combine them with Time Travel to expand the resonances even further. Traversing back in time five years and three parallel universes over to a coordinate of (–5,3) would provide for a significantly altered configuration of conscious expression.

Now, of course, a more accurate portrayal of this construct would be for the graph to be superimposed with torsion fields. The point (0,0) would represent the zero point of your heart space. Traversing horizontally toward the periphery of torsion fields would be Time Travel, and moving consciousness up or down in either direction of the torsion fields would represent parallel universes. Applying Time Travel and Parallel Universes together provides us with a fully flexible circumference of consciousness, which allows us to release what is limiting or no longer useful and expand our awareness into the full totality of our limitless selves.

NINE

The True Authentic Self and Perfectly Imperfect

Enlightenment means waking up to what you truly are and then being that. Realize and be, realize and be. Realization alone is not enough. The completion of Self-realization is to be, which means to act, do, and express what you realize. This is a very deep matter, a whole new way of life- living in and as reality instead of living out the programmed ideas, beliefs, and impulses of your dreaming mind. The truth is that you already are what you are seeking.

—Adyashanti, Emptiness Dancing

The topic of the self is one that could fill many *M-Joy Practically Speaking* books. It has already been the topic of thousands of books and spiritual teachings. Self-realization is a never-ending discovery process; it is the journey that we inevitably may all share together in our own unique ways. Spiritual teachers and authors have addressed the topic of self from a number of different perspectives. There is the view that we must dissolve all sense of self as a separate individual to find the true self as no-self. Another view is that we must dissolve all beliefs, thoughts, and attachments and only then will we meet our authentic self. And, of course, one of the most common stances is that we must entirely dissolve our ego to realize our true self. In a sense, these different approaches are similar in implying that something about us needs to change for us to meet our true self. What if that is not true, at all?

Perhaps we are here to learn, and so awakening to our core essence and our true nature as limitless beings is part of the process. Perhaps we came here to play, to experience joy, and to wonder/wander in the magnificence of this beautiful creation that is life. Perhaps the journey of life is the ongoing process of awakening to everything we are, by virtue of dissolving everything we are not, and then *choosing* for ourselves what to participate in. This last part is crucial: Choice. To make a choice. To choose.

We are all unique individuals, and yet we all stem from that which is all-inclusive of identity and also is totally void of identity. Perhaps enlightenment is recognizing divinity in everything as no-thing coupled with realizing that we can choose where to focus our awareness. We can choose what matters to us and what brings us joy. We can choose where we want to resonate. The power of choice is what gives rise to the rhythm of our individual and collective realities, because our choices determine our experiences.

In a universe of unlimited potential, our power of choice is a laser beam of light, shining upon us from universal consciousness to illuminate our dance. How we tango with the universe, our self, and others is an ongoing process of defining and refining our choices and actions. The movement begins from within the synchronicity of our hearts. Our hearts dance the eternal rhythm of joy. Choose joy.

True Authentic Self: Perfectly Imperfect

At the time this book began to percolate, guidance advised me to distinguish between authentic self and true authentic self. Initially, I did not understand the advice, and I thought perhaps it was redundant. What was the point, I wondered, of adding the word *true* in front of *authentic?* Only a few weeks later, I realized the significance of what was being gifted within those words.

Here is how our True Authentic Self (TAS) differs from our authentic self. Our TAS says, in effect, "I know

I am consciousness potential and a limitless being, and yet I coexist peacefully with my self-imposed limitations. I am unfolding daily in each moment, letting go of who I was a moment ago, so I can embrace more of who I am be-coming now." Authentic self embodies limitations. Our True Authentic Self (TAS) embodies both, limitlessness with limitations. Our TAS has limiting self-concepts that have been conditioned into personal awareness as well as presence and awareness of divine beingness, that which is unconditional love as coherent light. Within the TAS is a peaceful co-existence and synthesis without judgment. Our TAS is willing to explore parts of self that may not match the picture of limitless being, and it opens into these parts with equal love and light. Our TAS embraces the full totality of beingness and does not hide the yucky stuff from awareness.

Our True Authentic Self is perfectly imperfect.

The True Authentic Self (TAS) expands beyond the authentic self in that every moment is an opportunity to grow into more of what you are becoming, rather than remaining who you have been. It is not something that happens suddenly one day. It is a process that is always unfolding, refining, and expanding. The TAS stumbles, learns from the stumble, and gets right back up.

Our True Authentic Self is an evolving expression of coherency, congruency, and integrity in action. I define the *coherency* of True Authentic Self (TAS) as awareness of an unbroken connection to universal consciousness and limitless potential expressed as flow. *Congruency* is alignment of awareness of this coherent connection with everything *in relation to,* or relating to self. *Integrity* is the expression of coherency and congruency in all intentions and actions.

Integrity is a presence of heart and mind that responds honestly in the moment to what is, with full and abiding transparency. Our True Authentic Self (TAS) honors and values our own wants, needs, and desires as much as it does everyone else's, and it is not cloaked in programming, beliefs, opinions, and expectations. Our TAS knows that impositions of limitations are impostors.

As individuals, we can make a powerful choice to embrace integrity. When integrity is embodied, coherency invariably follows, as they are not mutually exclusive. Integrity creates a coherent field of connection established with all that is, allowing for all that we already are to unfold, with all that we are meant to *Be-come.*

Integrity Is Authenticity

The privilege of a lifetime is to become who you truly are.
—C. G. Jung

Integrity is authenticity. There is nothing to fear. Integrity is not some external standard that is incessantly beyond reach, or a mark that we will miss akin to SIN which is: Separate, Identify and Name. Integrity is within us, and is not something to earn. Like grace, it is freely available if we choose. Integrity is simply being wholly (who we truly are) without identifying ourselves exclusively through the masks and personas that we may hide behind.

Authenticity is not so scary. Many spend their whole lives running from themselves and hiding inherent greatness behind projections. Waking up to being exactly who we are, with total acceptance, can stop the exhausting marathon of avoidance. In the pause, if only for a moment, there is a meeting of the soul as our unique sole signature begins to express in an entirely new and liberated way. It becomes like breathing. Easy. Integrity, as authenticity, brings forth joy from within. Nothing to do other than to be, integrate (in-to-great), and express from that natural whole state.

TAS and *Self-Is*

Loving self is *self-is*. Our True Authentic Self (TAS) knows that loving and honoring self is *not* selfish. Rather, self-love is *self-is*. TAS recognizes self as a *direct extension* of universal consciousness, and that caring for oneself is a potent carrier wave for joy. When we appreciate our self in the myriad ways that honor our own needs and desires, love is amplified and more love becomes available for others. There is nothing selfish in loving self.

Heart-ily (Hardly) Selfish

Research conducted by Institute of HeartMath has shown that brain waves can entrain in the presence of another person's coherent heart field. This means that thoughts can be sensed and perceived by another when coherency is present. Furthermore, positive emotions such as love and appreciation, expressed in conjunction with a coherent heart field, are more likely to be picked up by another.

When we drop into our hearts while engaging in loving thoughts, our thoughts are amplified and conveyed to another through our coherent field. In other words, the synchrony and connection are extended beyond self to another. When we embody heart-centered awareness, our thoughts and emotions can favorably affect us as well as those around us. A ripple effect occurs when we live from our hearts first and allow our positive thoughts to follow.

When we love ourselves as we are, perfectly imperfect, and honor ourselves with loving thoughts and emotions, as well as with deeds of appreciation, our self-love radiates to others.

Love has many forms of expression, including the attributes of kindness, appreciation, caring, attention, and forgiveness. It is awesome to access love through

the field of the heart as a deeply impersonal, unconditional, cohesive force of universal consciousness.

Being, Not Un-doing

Our True Authentic Self does not require the total
dismantling of everything that is familiar. It allows us to
show compassion toward our own vulnerabilities in the
same way we are willing to show compassion to others.
Our TAS embraces love of self in its entirety—perfectly
imperfect—even the parts we do not like. As an absolutely unique expression of consciousness potential
whose core essence never changes, our True Authentic
Self is continually transforming, evolving, and letting go
of what is no longer useful. Our TAS embraces the
moment and says, "Here I am. Totally present. Right
now. I am different than I was a moment ago, and I look
forward to who I may be a moment from now."

Heart-centered awareness leads us to meet our True
Authentic Self. In that place of no space, we hear our
inner voice, the inner voice of the one who is genuinely
who we are.

When we meet our True Authentic Self, we may notice that, despite a knowingness that we are limitless
beings, we still are disentangling from our self-imposed
limitations. Our TAS can learn to recognize limitlessness
through the contrast of limitations, instead of seeing
them as mutually exclusive. Our TAS leverages contrast
as a trajectory for personal evolution.

Our TAS does not necessarily yield us a life of bliss
and sheer happiness all the time. In fact, fully embodying our TAS sometimes can yield quite the opposite
experience. It is at times lonely and miserable—and it is
never a permanent sense of being. It is always an im-
permanent sense of experience where we can be aware
that we are *not* the experience but rather, we are simply
having an experience as the experiencer. This distinction
is key and serves as a marker, reminding us to always

recognize that our true essence is that of a limitless being connected to universal consciousness.

There are times when I choose to go right smack into my perceived misery and wallow there for a bit to learn, evolve, transform, and make distinctions about my TAS, including the one that is having the experience that feels utterly miserable. There is nothing *right* or *wrong* about feeling miserable, either as a perception or as immersion in the experience. When we are miserable, it is not who we are, and as long as we remember that it truly is temporary, then it will be temporary. Or it may last until another day, because grace works that way, too. However, if we choose to identify closely with our misery, as if it were an intimate friend, then we lose sight of our essence, and our essence is not the misery. Misery is a choice. We may choose to become addicted to misery or to any experience.

When we feel we are drowning in any experience, life rafts are always available. We can choose to grab on to the many hands of grace that extend from those rafts and climb aboard to float with the current. Stormy seas, too, shall pass. Sometimes the swell seems just too big to handle, but we can float in our knowingness that the universe never gives us more than we can handle.

We are truly capable of so much more than we know, and sometimes that is what misery teaches us. Fighting the flow of misery, or the flow of any perceived negative emotion, will drown us if we resist the current. When we go with the flow of the experience, the experience can flow through us. As with any emotion (e-motion), the *energy-in-motion* will flow into tides of change.

Even amidst misery, we may find our joy, which heralds the recognition of what we truly are as limitless beings. This is a truth that our hearts have always known, and our True Authentic Self is continually remembering.

Joy for No Reason

Joy is available to us regardless of our circumstances. Circumstances are fleeting experiences that are subject to time and space. Joy is an ever-present essence that is found through our hearts in our inherent connection to universal consciousness. Joy is our natural state of being. When we embody the state of Joy with presence and consistency, then joy shimmers as a brilliant translucence in the intersecting waves of our reality.

There may always appear to be chaos, storms, challenges, complications, and distractions. These appearances can serve as attempts to thwart our natural state of being—that which is joy—which is available to us regardless of circumstances.

Appearances are deceiving to those who are perceiving. Sometimes things appear to fall apart, when they are virtually coming together. Virtual precedes actual. Trust in the virtue of what your heart knows and resonate with this knowingness always.

Sometimes we find joy when we least expect it: beneath the swell, in the storm, amidst the chaos. Joy is always there. Our challenge is to notice it is there when all else seems to indicate otherwise. For some, life is falling apart. To those in joy, life is perpetually falling together.

Drop into the field of the heart and find the essence of joy, ever-present in the calm sea of infinite potential. Hold space for what you desire and know in your heart that it is already done. Notice the space is a reservoir of grace pouring continuously into manifestations as experience.

Flow with Ego

Finding our true authentic self does not require total abandonment of ego. True Authentic Self (TAS) beckons us to accept ego and invites ego to follow along as the heart leads us into manifesting desires that consciousness is continually creating. Our TAS lives from the heart first in all endeavors and integrates ego as a useful expression of universal consciousness. EGO can be considered Energy Going Out, and it is a powerful tool for expression when it follows as an extension of the heart. Ego is like a puppy dog that desperately wants to run in the park. However, to allow him in the park without a leash would be careless, and he might get carried away alone by the ego-police. Initially, when puppy-ego is shown his leash, he whines, resists, barks, and attempts to hide under the couch. Soon enough, though, he realizes that if he wants to cruise the park and experience the sheer joy of running in the grass, he will need to choose to wear his leash and let heart lead him. Before we know it, doggie has his leash in his mouth and is proudly following where heart lets him roam. Our TAS plays synergistically with ego and recognizes appropriate scenarios for leashing and unleashing ego while the trusted heart always leads the way.

When we embrace ego as an extension of us, it simply *is* as a part of our continual unfolding. When ego is perceived as something to be destroyed or controlled, then it is still the idea of ego seeking to destroy itself. The more we battle ego, the more we are enslaved by the idea of ego. Constructs can constrict us. But, when constructs are integrated they can liberate us.

Integration: Synthesis of Heart-Mind

It occurs to me that the heart field functions like an internal and external GPS system for navigating through all consciousness terrain. The mind, as intellect, complements the heart by virtue of implementing the desires of the heart through intention as action.

According to Dr. Roland McCarty, Director of Research at the Institute HeartMath,

> coherence is a sort of sign-wave pattern or rolling-hill pattern in the heart's rhythm when we're in this optimal state. The heart's rhythm is reflecting the communication that's going on between the heart and the brain, something very deep that's going on in our physiology. The heart actually sends more information to the brain, neurologically speaking, than the brain to the heart.[1]

In the same way we may perceive the interconnected patterns of universal consciousness through synchronicity and flow, coherence is a measurable physiological effect that also reflects synchrony and flow within the various systems in the body. Integration and synthesis of all the interconnected systems of self, including thoughts and emotions, creates coherence. I consider this coherence to be a reflection of our universal connection as flow.

Accessing limitless potential includes leveraging all of the gifts that have been bestowed upon us by universal consciousness. While heart-centered awareness is a way of being that can allow for access to undifferentiated consciousness potential, unity, and wholeness, it is our intellect of mind that facilitates our ability to make choices. It is the intellect that provides perspective and makes distinctions.

Without the intellect, we would have to relearn that a door is a door every time we encountered one. The intellect is incredibly useful for navigating through three-dimensional reality. Without the intellect, we would not have the ability to make choices and to experience the textures of reality that give rise to contrast. Without intellect, we would not be able to choose to open the door and step into an expression of infinite potential.

When we make choices for ourselves with our intellect in the lead, rather than our heart, then we are leading based on limitations rather than unlimited potential. Integrating heart-centered awareness with the precision-like nature of the intellect provides for a powerful synergy that allows for a complete expression of our inherent power.

In ME, we teach that the field of the heart is the first point of awareness and that the intellect is the second point that extends from the all. Consider this an expression of the Two Point. In this sense, the Two Point becomes an ongoing conversation with universal consciousness, providing unlimited access that is powered by personal choices.

Alignment of heart with clear intention and deliberate action creates a coherent template for the manifestation of desired experiences.

The Institute of HeartMath theorizes that living consciously from the heart improves intuition, which leads to greater discernment when making choices.[2]

In other words, the more we live from our hearts, the easier it is to make decisions.

This is a funny paradox, because heart-centered awareness is what provides us access to infinite potential and limitless possibilities. We actually have more choices available to us, and yet, those options become easier to discern. How heartening!

Each time we wake up and discover our hearts, we find our authentic power, our authentic voice, our infinite potential, and all the resources necessary to become the change and transformation we desire to experience. It is exciting to be a part of the collective consciousness, and every single one of us matters in the shifting grid of transformational awareness. How thrilling to discover that choosing heart-centered awareness can make such a profound difference in our own lives as well as the lives of others.

What It Means to Work on Ourselves

One of the most common questions put forth by students that I've taught from around the world is, "How do I work on myself?" Believe it or not, we actually have been working on (playing with) ourselves throughout this entire book. We have been practicing the art and science of heart-centered awareness, letting go into the all, and expanding our awareness to recognize our inherent connectivity with universal consciousness. That's why I am addressing this question here, towards the end of the book rather than at the beginning.

When we recognize that every interaction is an opportunity to play with self, then we are *always, in all ways,* engaging in the self-transformation process. Nonetheless, students are often interested in learning specific ways for working on self.

Practical Play with Self

Here are some useful suggestions for working on the self.

Stop working on yourself and play!

First, jettison the idea of *working* on problems. Work is tiring. Everything we do when we step into the field of the heart is play. So, instead of working on self, choose to play. When we are playing with patterns in our awareness, rather than *working on* problems, our problems get bored from lack of attention and tend to find somewhere else to propagate. When we focus on our patterns as problems, unfortunately, our focus actually amplifies them and the problems get bigger. So playfulness is a great way to shift patterns without being in the problem-solution mindset, where our focus may cause our problems to increase.

So, jettison the idea of *working* on self. There is no self as something separate from the all, anyway. Choose play. It is so much easier and so freeing not to *work* on self, at all, but instead to *play.* Playing with unique patterns of information as expressions of consciousness potential makes it easier to access change in all ways.

PLAY is Potential Love Awaiting You—to join in the fun.

Choose to Play! Just Play!

Self as no other

I remind students there is no difference between working on self and working on others, except for the distinctions people themselves make that they are either playing with *self* or playing with an *other*. Sometimes we may *perceive* a distinction, thinking that we can't work on ourselves as easily as we may be able to work on another. As previously stated, the idea of *working* on self perpetuates the notion of *work* and *self* as constructs, which may limit what we easily notice. Go to the state of *PLAY* and enter the field of joy and miracles.

Remember, everything is a Two Point, a conversation with consciousness. The Two Point allows us to navigate in awareness between what we are noticing now and what we have yet to notice. It facilitates the establishment of resonance with a desired change or potential yet unrealized. So whether noticing on self or with another, the process is no different. We are still noticing what is different, not what is the same. It may *seem* more difficult to notice change in self for some people, because we are so habituated to noticing ourselves based on what we expect to see. It is a lot like looking in the mirror every day. We see what we expect to see and not what is really there. Thus, we may not notice the changes that are obvious to a neutral observer.

So how do you work on self? Consider setting it up in a way that allows you to circumvent perceived limitations you may be encountering. If you are conceivably (and/or perceivably) able to work (play) with others more easily than with self, set it up so that when you are playing with self, you are playing with another. In other words, see *your* patterns as though you were interacting with another's patterns and proceed in the same way you would play with others, or another other.

I like to create a hologram of myself so that I can see my patterns directly in front of me. This way I gain leverage into patterns as my own observer, rather than personalizing them. An observer vantage point really helps me perceive multiple options from a state of neutrality, which is definitely a key to the transformation process.

If you are not comfortable with a holographic construct, I suggest using a stuffed animal or a water bottle as a surrogate to represent you. Anything can represent self, and using an inanimate object in the universal hologram helps to support objective awareness.

A key component to leveraging any chosen inanimate object to represent self is to establish coherency with the all and then congruently connect with the inanimate object *as if* it actually is you. Then, drop into the field of the heart and notice what you notice. You may choose to do the Two Point, Time Travel, or Parallel Universe processes as tools for transformation. Then, maintain integrity with your surrogate connection by noticing what you notice within yourself that is different. Remember, notice what is different, not what is the same.

As you play with your patterns in the *virtual* hologram, what do you notice within you or around you that is different? Since the thought of the thing *is* the thing, deciding to work on an object as if it were self has the same effect as working directly on your body. There is no difference. In the hologram, everything is connected. Anything can represent you because you decide that it does. You can choose.

Just choose and PLAY. Choose and PLAY.

Remember that, at the level of the field, each time we play with others we are actually playing with self. Every person who *consciously* shows up in our resonant reality is a reflection of some aspect of ourselves. This means that every Two Point you do on another is a Two Point on self. This may be my favorite aspect of working in a field of consciousness potential, for in the giving *is* the receiving. The field of infinite possibilities benefits everyone who chooses to play.

Because we are *not* running energy, there is no energy drain on self when playing on another. Remember, we are connecting to information as potential to establish resonance, and what is expressed is energy. So, playing in the field is not tiring, at all. In addition, there is no limit to what is possible for us when we work on others, because there is no other and there is no self. There is only the field of consciousness potential, awaiting our recognition. All is available for everyone to experience, as we drop into our hearts and notice options.

Continue playing and notice that any perceived problem is really an opportunity for the field to teach you how to navigate more fluidly so that you can access more of your own inherent potential.

In-Joy!

TEN

Relationships
Co-Creation, Unification,
and Ripples in the Pond

> *What we call our destiny is truly our character and that character can be altered. The knowledge that we are responsible for our actions and attitudes does not need to be discouraging, because it also means that we are free to change this destiny. One is not in bondage to the past, which has shaped our feelings, to race, inheritance, background. All this can be altered if we have the courage to examine how it formed us. We can alter the chemistry provided we have the courage to dissect the elements.*
>
> *—Anaïs Nin*

All that you experience is you *in relation to*—everything!

This whole book is about relating. Relating is a dynamic, ever-evolving essential of relationships. Relating describes you *in relation to*. Relating is you *in relation to* universal consciousness and its infinite potential. Relating is you *in relation to*—everything! As an extension of universal consciousness, that which you create is connected to the all and is experienced wholly *in relation to* you! Everything is in relationship. Everything is you in-relation, too.

Pebble in a Pond

Your perceived personal reality can be likened to a pebble dropping into a pond. The pebbles represent your choices. The pond represents universal consciousness. Wherever you choose to drop pebbles into the pond creates a ripple effect that emanates in all directions, reverberating through *every-thing in relation to* your choices. The pebbles create the ripples. In turn, the ripples respond to your pebbles. So, your choices determine where the pebble drops into the pond, and there is a ripple effect that is the holographic placeholder for your interactive reality-creation.

When, through heart-centered awareness, you shift how you show up, everything shifts around you. For example, if you want to change how you relate to your family, how a person relates to you, or even how your garden blooms *in relation to* you, you can shift your awareness and resonance with respect to where you choose to drop your pebbles into the pond. The ripple effect of everything *in relation to* you changes according-ly. Shifting awareness is a really empowering way to access change without really doing anything other than noticing what you notice from your heart, and then choosing how to show up *in relation to* ... everything. Just choose.

Exponents of Grace

There's a component to the field of the heart that can be amplified or multiplied when it is coupled with compo-nents of grace. This component of the heart field can be expressed as a mathematical equation for accessing personal power, wherein the Heart Field × Grace = Exponential Personal Power:

$$HF \times G = EPP$$

As with any mathematical equation, the components of grace can be revealed in multiple directions. Any component of personal power, when divided by grace, can summate (consummate), or bring together, the various functions of the field of the heart. They are interrelated, interconnected, interdependent, symbiotic, synergistic, synchronistic, tessared, and torsioned together.

When we embody personal power and access the field of the heart, we are accessing grace, as well. These three components work synergistically. Thus, accessing the field of the heart accesses grace and also accesses personal power.

Personal power tends to evoke different references for different individuals, based on their prior experiences with power. Personal power, as a function of grace, is not power over anything or anyone. Personal power is instead a power that comes from direct access to the field of the heart and the infinite potential that is available when we plug into the grid of universal consciousness potential. Within a heart-centered connection, there is nothing to be powerful or to be powering over.

Grace is a stance of inner power that does not control. Rather, grace is a gentle-handed command from the heart field. Grace is an inner strength, an inner solitude, and an inner knowing; it is a centering that provides balance for every dance of awareness, for every interaction, and for every relationship to anyone or anything. Through grace, each movement in our reality becomes an expression of the field of the heart, an expression of grace, and an expression of personal power.

Grace itself is both unifying and relational, in that the experience of grace reminds us of the inherent connectivity between everything and everyone. We can see that the experience of grace is often expressed through our intimate relations with one another.

Grace as Intimacy (in-to-me-see)

One of your most important intimate relationships is the one you have with yourself. The relationship with yourself is you *in relation to* you. You *in relation to* you is an eternal marriage between the True Authentic Self and your heart. The vows are simple and profoundly meaningful. Commit to love, honor, and listen to yourself through your heart, in sickness and in health, for richer

145

or poorer, in death you'll not part. Vow to appreciate, encourage, and support yourself when you need it most, and even when you do not need it. Promise to always be honest with yourself and to express your truth as it occurs to you. When you forget any of these promises, remember the premise of forgiveness, as forgiveness is an ever-evolving gift of grace. Very important in this marriage with yourself is to find your Joy. Be Joy. Live Joy. In-Joy! Love self first and foremost, and from there, love exponentially. Love is the ripple-effect.

The Function of Love

In *Love without End,* Glenda Green speaks eloquently about the scientific function of love:

> If you would think upon the function of love scientifically, think of it as reversal-transference—a point of function where two complementary forces, in the presence of a third stabilizing factor, exchange modes and one becomes the other. This is primary magnetism and compression. . . . This is also the mystery of paradox, which precedes, supersedes, exceeds, and reconciles all patterns of structure into simple fluidity.
>
> A whole is designated by its character and quality — not by its boundaries! Its center, however, can be marked with a "0." The forces expanding from that point exponentially multiply the energy released. Simultaneously, through the aspect of energetic tension, energy is transferred from one extreme of expansion to another. By these reversals, torque is generated, and that sets in motion a magnetic spin, or vortex.[1]

Zero-ing in on Love

The center of a whole can be marked by Zero. Zero has infinite value: Consider unconditional love as consciousness potential, represented by the placeholder Zero. Zero is *not* nothing, as in *without value.* Zero is *nothing;* whole and all-inclusive of all values and expressions. Zero is, perhaps, empty space that is voluminous with potential. As nothing, Zero has no boundaries, no parameters, and no perspectives. It is a Zero-point field of infinite consciousness potential.

One Love IS

One is a placeholder for universal consciousness. One *is* universal consciousness, expressing from consciousness potential, represented through Zero. One is part of Zero and contains all of Zero, but One is not greater than Zero. From Zero, as *no-thing,* comes *something,* and that *something* is One, as the all.

Unconditional love (Zero-point field as consciousness potential) expressed as One, may be considered *conditional* or *conditioned* by virtue of the parameters it has chosen. Parameters chosen are One. Just One.

Except for One being *all-inclusive,* which it is, there are really no other boundaries. *All-inclusive* means infinite inclusion, infinite expansion, infinite possibilities, and infinite expressions. Therefore, to me, One is *still* unconditional love. One *is.* Love *is.* One *is.*

Love IS

One, as Love IS, seeks to know itself in the same way that consciousness potential seeks expression. In other words, Love IS, in its stillness as unconditional love, has no way of knowing itself as love without experiences that reflect back its own essence to itself.

As One, Love IS, in its stillness as unconditional love, dances alone—until its movements emulate a spin or torsions of joy, dancing through *is*-ness.

Love spins and spins, and in its spinning there is a momentum that creates and propagates another torsion field. Another torsion field manifests as a reflection of itself, such that the torsion fields can now dance together.

In this reflection, there is a coupling, a relationship-*to*. Love IS, as One, sees itself mirrored in another. Awareness of self is born *in relation to* another. One, as unconditional love, spins gracefully into a new condition or expression of love, as Two.

Two is not greater than One, just as One is not greater than Zero. All are inherently connected. Each seemingly separate, albeit truly connected, part contains the whole of each *One* and *Zero* too (*Two*)!

Love IS, love expresses, love experiences, and love reflects. Love returns to itself. Love IS. As love, you are, you express, you experience, and you reflect. You return to yourself as love because love is what you are. Love is what we all are. We are . . . I am . . . and you are All that IS.

Love IS, 'I AM'

The 'I AM' is a cohesive, magnetic connection of love. It is through the I AM *in relation to* others that we readily notice and experience the torsion fields of love, spinning as grace.

Self *in relation to* others offers a plethora of opportunities; opportunities for growth and understanding of our True Authentic Self, as infinite beings peacefully co-existing within our own perceived limitations. Self *in relation to* others is a magnificent, dynamic field in which to experience the limitless power of the unconditional love that is universal consciousness. Similarly, being *in relation to* others offers a *perfectly imperfect* playing field to experience limitation through relationship. What a wonderful way to reconcile and unify any perceived disparities within ourselves! Love IS and love relates.

In relation to, grace abounds.

I Love You *and* . . .

Love IS because unconditional love has no boundaries. Unconditional love is without conditions. Unconditional love does not mean loving all conditions. Many mistake the notion of unconditional love to mean tolerating intolerable circumstances. This is not so. Unconditional love is Love IS. Unconditional love *in relation to* another does not mean conditions are placed on the love itself. It means conditions are placed upon the circumstances in which we *are willing to* or *not willing to*, or *choose to* or *choose not to* participate in. Unconditional love is clearly:

"I love you *and* the circumstances are not in integrity for me."

"I love you *and* I am not congruent with these behaviors."

"I love you *and* I do not agree with your choices, so I choose to participate in something different."

"I love you *and* this pattern is okay."

"I love you *and* I choose to stand beside you."

"I love you *and*—no."

"I love you *and*—yes."

Loving unconditionally does not require us to relinquish our personal power, our integrity, or our self-respect to prove something. Love has nothing to prove. It is already wholly proven. Love just *is*. Unconditional love says, "I love you *and* I don't need you (or me) to *prove* that I can love unconditionally."

Love Is Void of Manipulation

All men and women are connected by an energy which many people call love, but which is, in fact, the raw material from which the universe was built. This energy can not be manipulated, it leads us gently forwards, it contains all we have to learn in this life. If we try to make it go in the direction we want, we end up desperate, frustrated, disillusioned, because that energy is free and wild.

—Paulo Coelho, The Zahir

Loving unconditionally is *not* love as manipulation. Manipulation is not loving. Manipulation is twisting love to meet an agenda, such that the love is siphoned off into a constrictive funnel called *agenda*. Clear the agenda! Love is free of agenda.

Loving unconditionally also means we do not subject ourselves to the manipulations of others. Manipulation is a method of attempting to use love to *suck* power. Manipulation is a power struggle and a drain on our resources.

Love is its own power source. Succumbing to manipulation may seem easier than saying, "I love you *and* no thank you." Placating a manipulator may temporarily alleviate the energetic drain, but at a vibrational level, placating manipulation simply feeds manipulation rather than offering awareness of different options. In technical terms, a relationship in which partners use manipulation to respond to manipulation may be described as a passive-aggressive relationship. Love does not manipulate. Love IS.

Manipulation of love is a form of addiction. It is reliance upon another person, or people, for power, using their love and adoration as energy and as a *means to an end*, rather than connecting directly to the unconditional love of universal consciousness that is one's own infinite source.

We can either nourish ourselves in Love IS, or we can continue to feed our addictions to manipulation. Denial is the finger on an invisible hand that maneuvers us, too. End the denial and the addictions to manipulation, and we find ourselves cradled in the hands of love.

When we drop down into the heart, we can recognize manipulation in ourselves, and others, through the innate knowingness of the heart. There is an air of pretension when we encounter manipulation. We feel it. Pretension, as a *precursor to tension*, which can lead to uneasy feelings, and even dis-ease. When we *end the pretend* in the manipulative behaviors, we may also *end what portends us.*

Done Is Done

Loving unconditionally means we may encounter various levels of *done in relation to* others' patterns. Part of loving unconditionally means simply being done with a relationship in its current configuration.

Love never goes anywhere. Only the circumstances change. When we realize this, loving unconditionally is easier, because there is nothing to lose. Free from fear of perceived loss and free from judgment, we can navigate clearly and make choices based on love, not fear. Love IS, and it is always there.

What Is Done?

What is *done? Done* is done, and done can surface in many ways.

At a transformative level, *done* means the patterns that we were entangled with, or that were preventing us from loving unconditionally, have been released. There is nothing to hang onto any longer. There are no attachments in unconditional love, as Love IS already complete and whole in its magnificent and absolute simplicity. When we release our attachments to perceived complications, the complications let go of their attachments to us.

True Authentic Relating (TAR)

Being *done* with a relationship in its current configuration does not necessarily mean that the relationship is over. Instead, it may mean that True Authentic Relating (TAR) has come to light. *Done* may serve as an opportunity to honestly communicate wants, needs, and desires to others without attachments to their response. True Authentic Relating is a congruent expression of coherency by our True Authentic Self. In other words, TAR is maintaining awareness of an unbroken connection to all and aligning awareness toward others in a manner that reflects this connection. True Authentic Relating is *integrity-in-action*. True Authentic Relating (TAR) represents *clear intent* and *right relations*.

Love as an Offering

When one offers love freely and unconditionally to another and it is rejected, that is not a rejection of self. Rather, it is a reflection of another's own limited awareness in rejection of the inherent love that they are.

When we extend love to another, that love is an invitation and an offering for higher awareness. Loving unconditionally—without attachments to whether that love is received, accepted, or reciprocated—plants seeds that can blossom in unexpected ways. Love IS and does not require another to accept it for the love that is to grow. Where love is, love grows.

Unconditional Love as Compassion

Loving unconditionally means we are compassionate and empathetic *in relation to* others, but we are not necessarily sympathetic. Let me explain.

Merriam-Webster defines *sympathy* as

> an affinity, association, or relationship between persons or things wherein whatever affects one similarly affects the other . . . mutual or parallel susceptibility or a condition brought about by it or . . . an inclination to think or feel alike.

Energetically, sympathy is entraining to another's resonant vibration. But, we do not want or need to enmesh ourselves in someone else's stuff. Practically speaking, when someone is miserable and we sympathize, we are likely to become miserable, too.

Empathy, on the other hand, is defined by *Merriam-Webster* as

> the action of understanding, being aware of, being sensitive to, and experiencing the feelings, thoughts, and experience of another of either the past or present without having the feelings, thoughts, and experience fully communicated in an objective manner . . . also: the capacity for this.

Compassionate empathy arises when we connect our resonant vibration with source, expressing through us as love and coherent light, and then align our awareness to the resonance of another. Then, when *they* are experiencing misery, we are embodying and radiating joy. In turn, the joy that we are expressing reverberates toward them. If they choose not to receive it, then we are still able to have a joy-filled experience, with or without them.

Loving unconditionally does not mean we must become *miserable* to help *someone who is resonating misery.* We can create leverage and wiggle room so that the pattern of misery can change if we simply shine our light as love.

In recognition that the terms compassion, empathy, and sympathy are nominalizations and somewhat subjective, I offer the following personal distinction that has helped me immeasurably when interacting with others.

As an empath, I am quite adept at tracking and following individual and group energetic patterns. Initially, when I first began teaching large groups, I was quite *sympathetic* to everyone and left interactions shrouded in *other people's stuff.* I felt everything from ecstatic bliss to suicidal depression, and it was exhausting, confusing, cumbersome, and not very fun. (Note: We are all empathic, but some are more attuned to this part of awareness than others.)

I found it useful to make a distinction between *sympathy* and *compassionate empathy.* Sympathy entailed

noticing another's experience while aligning my vibration to the resonant information and vibration in which
they were experiencing reality. If they were sad, hurt, or
triggered, I felt the same. I felt what they felt; it was
stifling to me. There was hardly any leverage to notice
anything beyond their perceived experience. Sympathy
offered little in the way of accessing possibilities.

Alternatively, *compassionate empathy* allows me to
align my vibration with source first, through my heart
field. I must say that this has proven very re-source-full!

From a state of infinite potential, when aligning and
connecting our awareness *in relation to others,* we can
remain coherent with source while still being able to
notice, track, and follow others' experiences and vibrations. Compassionate empathy, as an extension of
source, is an inclusive *being-ness* that allows us to notice
and experience, with others, from a space of grace.

So, distinguishing between *sympathy* and *empathy
with compassion* enables us to retain a locus of command
with limitless possibilities while still honoring and
leveraging the inherent connectivity that we all have
with one another.

Neutrality Is Compassionate Relating

Neutrality encompasses *compassionate empathy* and is an
integral part of relating through heart-centered awareness. Neutrality is sometimes referred to as detachment.
I prefer not to associate the word *detachment* with the
word *neutrality,* because detachment sometimes implies
disconnection from something. I prefer using the word
neutrality to mean or represent *new-to-reality.*

When experiencing *neutrality,* we perceive the world
through a lens of innocent perception, free from judg-
ments and still connected to the all. We are most compassionate when our vibration is aligned, with passion,
to that which is *all* as universal consciousness.

Heart-centered awareness is *all*-inclusive and includes everything, so there is nothing to attach to or detach from in relating to others. Compassion is found in the field of the heart. Compassion is connection to source while observing through awareness from a space of completion.

Neutrality does not mean, "I do not care." It means, "I am inherently connected to everything, and that means everything is available to me."

Neutrality creates a *portal-to-unity*, an opportunity to transcend our perceived limitations. Neutrality is an extension of oneness and provides us with the leverage for something to change. Being neutral is a compassionate form of caring when we are relating to one another.

Reflections on Projections

We may come to know ourselves through the reflections of others.

When these reflections from others are not accurate, we can forget who we truly are. When, instead, these reflections are projections of distorted perceptions, we may encode information that does not match our limitless essence.

Often this occurs during our formative years *in relation to* our parents and guardians. As little ones, we do not yet see ourselves as separate from those who are caring for us. Their thoughts and emotions become our thoughts and emotions. Their limited perspectives become our limited perspectives. Often, in their confusion and sense of separation from source as universal consciousness and its infinite potential, they unknowingly project their perceptions of themselves onto their children.

These projections include, but are not limited to, their own limiting programs and memes. For example, if they feel they are not good enough, or not deserving, they may project their thoughts and feelings onto others.

These imprints encode with information that causes children to feel *not good enough* or *not worthy enough,* and ultimately it creates feelings and experiences of not being loved unconditionally.

As a result, these experiences can establish patterns for a lifelong path of dysfunction and dis-ease, often through addiction. Addictions become placeholders in awareness to fill the early experience of not feeling loved unconditionally. All addictions are an unfulfilling quest for unconditional love.

Addicted to Love

Patterns of addiction are an attempt to find True Authentic Self and simultaneously to avoid it. The placeholder that the addiction represents serves as a habituated strategy to avoid recognizing self as an infinitely whole, perfect, and limitless being having an experience of limitation. The pattern as placeholder serves as a habituated strategy to seek fulfillment and acceptance of TAS in something outside of self that is inherently and incessantly empty.

Is addiction a dis-ease? Well, yes, there is a lack of ease in chronic avoidance. However, classified as a disease in allopathic terms, the behavior of the individual will likely conform to the conventional outcomes for the established morphic field. There is little wiggle room available to heal from a disease that, in allopathic terms, *has no cure.* In many allopathic models, once an addict, always an addict. But addiction is not an identity. Addiction is a conditioned behavior. A person with an addiction or who is considered an addict—is *not* his addiction.

Seeing addiction for what it is, and nourishing the person in a clarifying way rather than feeding the confused pattern, changes the configuration. Reflections that nurture the person and not the addiction provide care that allows the long-standing patterns of addiction to stand down and release.

Projections can create confusion and can also lead to other dysfunctional behaviors and dis-eases. For example, many autoimmune disorders may be placeholders that reflect *self not recognizing self.*

Being held and nurtured literally, figuratively, or energetically in a space of unconditional love allows for a release of addictive or confused patterns, which may lead to dis-ease, such that a return to wholeness is recognized, activated, and realized.

Healer as Whole: Trance to Transform

Healer heal thyself is a popular meme that is sometimes interpreted as "I cannot fully help others to heal or transform until I heal myself."

Conversely, we may out-loop or project our own desire to transform ourselves onto those we are *in relation to* personally and professionally. We may neglect to attend to ourselves, at the exclusion of helping another. In the giving is receiving. However we must choose to receive, too.

At a certain level of awareness, there is no healing or transforming of self or other. There is only awareness of the various distinctions we believe may stand in the way. Healing and transformation is an ongoing journey with an unlimited depth of potential and expression. When we get out of our own way, our limitless potential becomes available. Healer as whole. Healee as whole. The hole in whole is already complete. When we transform ourselves, the world around us changes. Transformation, through love, is the ripple effect.

Be Your Own Light!

It can sometimes feel challenging to radiate light when we appear to be surrounded by projections and shadows of negativity. Yes, it may seem easier to blend in with the reflections and crevices of confusion rather than to keep shining. Yet, to be a beam of coherent light in a seemingly dark jungle is what allows illuminating awareness to be revealed, recognized, and to ripple into reality. It's akin to being the *one-hundredth monkey* who illuminates the other ninety-nine monkey-minds to realize, "Aha! I see you now, as you have always seen me, and now I see myself, too. I no longer need to snuff your light so I can feel comfortable. I no longer need your projection to know myself. I know that I am light by my reflection. I know I am light because it is all I see."

Choosing Love as Protection

When we do find ourselves in a reality subset that says we need protection, then our perception needs protection, too. As long as we believe we need protection, we will need protection. Protection is a matter of resonant vibration. Where we resonate, so we shall experience.

There is occasionally value in a perspective of protection. When in a resonant vibration, density, layer, or pattern of consciousness that warrants protection, then use it. Or modify your resonance and take the elevator to a different floor of awareness.

Sometimes love wears a raincoat to get through a storm. What works optimally is *awareness,* and protection is simply an extension of awareness. I speak not in theory but based on experience, having navigated through tens of thousands of complex terrains of consciousness. Sometimes, I dress my awareness in a raincoat to navigate more proficiently and efficiently through a pattern. When the perceived storm is over, I remove the raincoat. In other words, protection is a temporary layer of consciousness that can be worn to weather a storm. The sunshine and light always return.

At a certain level of consciousness, it is *all* us, as we are *all*. From that level of connection, there is nothing to protect against, as we are not in need of protecting us from ourselves. We are the dark energy that has distanced us from our own light. We are the demon we may recognize in another. Everything we see is a reflection of us.

We are that which is all, which is source, which is everything, and when we recognize this, we can shape our perceptions to flexibly navigate through terrains of consciousness so that there is no fear. This is a form of modifying resonance. Resonate with a knowing that, in the field of the heart, there is only consciousness potential awaiting recognition.

Practical Play: Modifying Resonance

If you do find yourself perceiving a need for protection, see yourself inside a pink bubble of unconditional love, and then invite that bubble to expand to include all that you notice.

Let Love Out

Relating to ourselves and others is an ongoing process of noticing and experiencing, being and doing. Love IS, and love is what we do. We recognize the inherent interconnectivity of all that is through the cohesive tapestry of love in our relationships. The tapestry of love is intricately spun with threads of grace. Through grace, our relationships with ourselves and others are continual, gifted opportunities to trance-form, and to evolve into clear reflections of our true essence: Love. Love is always available to us. Love is not something we need to earn or somehow let into our lives, because love is what we are. Let love out. When we let love out, the ripple effect impacts everyone on the planet. When we let love out, there is a dance of grace that touches the shared heart of one as all.

Desire for Love

All relationships carry with them an inherent desire to remain in a state of love. As love itself is boundless, free, and is always moving and flowing, containing a state of love within the fixed boundaries of a relationship can lead to feelings of restriction and dissatisfaction, rather than growth and satiation. More important, when we look to others as the source for the love we desire, we are forever seeking an elusive state. Seeking love from others to fulfill us, or to fully fill us, will likely leave us feeling empty.

When we stop looking outside ourselves for the level of love we desire and instead realize that we are a source of love, than we can shift how we show up, and then, inevitably, everything shifts around us. When we look to ourselves for the fulfillment of love, we quite naturally attract circumstances that reflect similar states of being. In turn, our relationships become more fulfilling, as they become an extension of that which is already full and whole in us. There is a freedom and an expansion found in loving self that allows for more love to flow to us and through us from all directions. This love is within us and is realized all around us. When we let love out *and* we let love in, the ripple effect expands exponentially through reciprocal waves of grace. When we let love in and let love out, we flow with grace, in an eternal, rhythmic dance of joy.

All in Grace

Grace is relational and is reflected in all our experiences. Grace is the expression of the unconditional love that is universal consciousness. Grace is the spinning of torsion fields in matter and experience. Grace is consciousness reinventing itself in every moment. Grace is our eternal float when stormy seas abound. Grace carries us, as we find our joy, as we remember who we are, as we embrace our truth. When we drop down into the field of our heart, grace is always with us. Grace is the calm unity we feel *in relation to* others, and when we see ourselves through the eyes of love. Grace is love dancing with all possibilities equally, and grace is yours for the asking. Let go into grace. Trust that grace will be with you always on your journey. Allow grace to express freely in all that you notice.

With grace, I thank you all for sharing this journey with me, through the field of the heart to discover our infinite potential. May you continue to explore what is possible and to experience the wonder of miracles every day, in practical play.

Practically speaking, in a *perfectly imperfect* way, I express appreciation for all that you already are and all that you are destined to become, as they are the same.

With love always and eternally In-Joy.

—Melissa Joy

ELEVEN

Delightful Delineations and Distinctions

Chapter 11 might at first glance appear to be a traditional glossary, but it is much more than that. Chapter 11, which contains delineations and distinctions I have made throughout the book, will serve as useful, quick references as you continue your journey through universal consciousness and its infinite potential. Some terms are a review of what you have already learned. Others contain expanded descriptions of constructs that invite you to further explore what these notions mean to you.

None of the terms included in this chapter are to be considered absolute. Rather, they are relative descriptions that offer you the opportunity to deepen your awareness of the expansive process that is interactive reality-creation.

Each term can be defined in many ways. I have chosen to define many based on what seems true for me. I invite you to absorb what is useful and expand your own understanding further. As we are ultimately the meaning-makers in terms of how we choose to interpret information, I offer the following meanings for your curiosity, ease, and flow toward your own meaning, however that may occur to you. In-Joy.

Abundance. A state of consciousness. A currency of infinite potential, expressing as flow. Abundance is a state of being or resonant vibration that lacks nothing. Resonate with abundance, and abundance flows into all that you are and all that you do. The essence of abundance is the recognition that all is available.

Acceptance. Allowance for *what is,* through neutrality, to facilitate change. Letting go of resistance to anything.

Addiction. A placeholder in awareness that represents an attempt to find True Authentic Self (TAS) and simultaneously avoid it. The placeholder that the addiction pattern represents serves as a habituated strategy to avoid recognizing self as an infinitely whole, perfect, and limitless being having an experience of limitation. The pattern as placeholder serves as a habituated strategy to look for fulfillment and acceptance of TAS in something outside of self that is inherently and incessantly empty. In this recognition, there is freedom to recondition awareness and embrace integrity. There is freedom to move from dis-ease to flow in total acceptance, to choose anew. Just choose.

All. Everything in totality. All is impersonal in nature and extends far beyond individual awareness, beyond the fabric of space-time, and beyond anything we may think we know definitively. Universal consciousness is all. In its entirety, it is void of perspective and identity because it includes all vantage points as part of itself. All is Love, and Love is all. (*See also* Universal consciousness)

Allowance. A state of acceptance that provides for a natural letting go of any negative charge that keeps our perspective on our reality locked into the polarity and duality of what we are attempting to discharge or transcend. In other words, a state of acceptance and allowance releases the unwanted charge against anything. (*See also* Acceptance)

Association memes. Memes that have been conceptually fused in our awareness. They are a bit like attitudes, because the presence of one meme triggers a thought or an emotion or another meme.[1]

Biophotons. Light emissions. It has been scientifically proven that every cell in the body emits more than one hundred thousand light impulses or photons per second. These light emissions, found in all living things, have been found to be the driving mechanism behind all biochemical reactions.[2]

Carrier wave. An electromagnetic wave that can be modulated in frequency, amplitude, or phase to transmit speech, music, images, or other signals.

Change. To make or become different. Change is a constant. The nature of change is flow. Change happens naturally when we are no longer resistant to *what is* and when we are no longer pushing against something or someone in an attempt to create transformation. (*See also* Transform)

Choice. Our inherent ability to choose where to resonate in our awareness. The power of choice creates the rhythm of our individual and collective realities. Our choices determine our experiences.

Choose. The process of aligning awareness with a possibility state to establish resonance so that a possibility becomes a probability that expresses as experience. Just choose.

Choose, notice, let go, allow, trust, choose. A method for experiencing change. *Choose* a pattern that you want to change or manifest. Drop down into the field of the heart and *notice* the connection to the all that is universal consciousness. *Let go* and release all attachment to and resistance to change. Let go into neutrality, which is a portal-to-unity (o-port-unity) with the all. *Allow* the pattern you noticed to exist in your awareness while also noticing the presence of other possibilities. *Trust* what you notice as you notice what is different, not what is the same. *Choose* where you want to resonate. Choose In-Joy.

Coherence. A correlation between the phases of two or more waves so that interference effects may be produced between them. Also, coherence is a correlation between the phases of parts of a single wave.

The Institute of HeartMath states:

> Heart coherence, marked by coherent, or smooth and balanced heart rhythms, is the optimal state for your heart, mind and emotions and all of the processes in your body, including cognitive, hormonal, digestive, respiratory and immune systems.[3]

Coherence is a unified field of undifferentiated consciousness potential that has not been defined or formed. It is also used to describe an unbroken connection with universal consciousness. For example, when we are in heart-centered awareness, we are easily able to access a state of coherence with universal consciousness, which may be observed by feelings of joy, connectivity, and synchronicity. Coherence is a reflection of our universal connection as flow. (*See also* Decoherence)

Collapse of the wave function. Simply stated, scientists were interested in exploring the nature of an electron and wanted to determine whether it was a particle or a wave. When they were in the room observing the electron, it behaved as a particle, which conformed to their expectations. When scientists left the room and videotaped the electron without observing it, the electron behaved like an indiscriminate wave. Scientists concluded that the expectations of the researchers had *collapsed the wave function*, changing the probable wave states to particle-based fixed forms. They concluded that, indeed, the consciousness of the observer collapses the wave function.

In our personal awareness, the collapse of the wave function means that our observations and expectations actually influence the apparent behavior of reality. This understanding empowers us to play with interactive reality-creation. Reality is neither particle nor wave. It is both and neither simultaneously, and as co-creators with universal consciousness, we are influencing how reality shapes itself.

Collective consciousness. The condition of the individual within the whole of society and how any given individual comes to view themself as a part of any given group. Specifically, the term has been used by social theorists/psychoanalysts like Durkheim, Althusser, and Jung to explain how an autonomous individual comes to identify with a larger group/structure. Definitively, *collective* means "formed by a collection of individual persons or things; constituting a collection; gathered into one; taken as a whole; aggregate, collected." *Consciousness* is more complex and harder to define in all its implications. *The Oxford English Dictionary* defines it as "joint or mutual knowledge; internal knowledge or conviction; knowledge as to which one has the testimony within oneself, esp. of one's own innocence, guilt, deficiencies," and as "the state or fact of being mentally conscious or aware of anything."

By combining the two terms, we can surmise that the phrase *collective consciousness* implies internal knowledge or a consciousness shared by a plurality of persons. The easiest way to think of collective consciousness, even with its extremely loaded historical content, is to regard it as being an idea or proclivity that we all share.

Compartmentalization (*also* compartmentalize or *come-apart-mental-lies*). Segregation and delineation of aspects of our awareness, producing a lack of integration, synchronization, harmony, and flow in our life.

Compartmentalization of our spiritual journey occurs when anything we consider *spiritual* is siphoned off from other various facets of our experienced reality. Any delineation made between spiritual and practical—or between spiritual and physical, mental, emotional, relational, or financial—are somewhat arbitrary. Such delineations become true when we resonate with them as if they were separate categories of consciousness. In a sense, all categories or compartments are memes, most of which have corresponding global morphic fields.

Because spirit is infused in everything, compartmentalizing spirit essentially means segregating that which is the all from itself. Yet, it is not possible to compartmentalize spirit. Spirit is not about anything, as it is everything *and* nothing. We can only compartmentalize our ideas about spirit. Consciousness as spirit, source, nature, field, love, light, or whatever we want to call it, does not discriminate. Spirit includes everything, including duality with its seemingly discrete polarities. Spirit, consciousness—whatever you call it—just *is*. When we cease to compartmentalize, then "come apart the mental lies" we have told ourselves about our limitations versus what is infinitely possible. Spirit has no limits, and neither do we.

Compassion and completion. Found within True Authentic Self (TAS), a combined state of being that transcends the perceived need for comparison and competition with others. When we show ourselves compassion, and honor the completion that is inherently within us all, then we are no longer driven to project our sense of lack onto others; we no longer compare and compete to feel worthy. In this recognition of our TAS, we end the self-betrayal and befriend the world.

Compassionate empathy. Entraining our resonant vibration to source, which expresses through us as love and coherent light, and then aligning awareness to another's resonance. When the other is experiencing misery and we are embodying and radiating joy, then the joy that we are reverberates and influences their state.

Congruence. Alignment of the awareness of our coherent connection with everything that relates to self.

Consciousness. Per *Merriam-Webster Dictionary*, the quality or state of being aware, especially of something within oneself; the state or fact of being conscious of an external object, state, or fact." Therefore, that which is conscious has perspective when observing what it perceives. As defined in this book, consciousness includes everything and excludes nothing. It does not stem from the universe, but instead, it is understood here that the universe stems from consciousness. Consciousness is all. (*See also* Universal consciousness)

Consciousness potential. As used in this book, consciousness potential is *no-thing* because it has not yet expressed itself as something. Consciousness potential is universal consciousness *before* consciousness creates, actualizes, and/or experiences. Consciousness potential is void of distinctions or boundaries, and therefore, it also has no limitations. Undifferentiated consciousness potential is limitless, formless, weightless, timeless, without space, without thought, and totally free. Consciousness potential is unconditional love before love expresses through conditions.

Constructs. Configurations of information contained or held in a specific form. Examples of constructs of consciousness include, but are not limited to, ideas, opinions, and beliefs.

Containers. Constructs of information that gives shape and form to an experience. Examples of containers are morphic fields, memes, masks, and personas.

Contrast. A calibration through which light, as awareness, notices its own movement. Through this awareness, light grows into more light, shining bright for the benefit of all. We can learn the most about our own light, vibration, and potential through contrast. Contrast allows for the cultivation of awareness between two states: the inertia and stagnation of perceived darkness (light distanced from itself) and the momentum and expansion of light as love. As we perceive the contrast, light is actually able to launch its momentum further.

In other words, the more light we shine into the shadows or darkness we perceive, the less the shadows or darkness affect us. By perceiving the contrast, we gain awareness and awaken to our True Authentic Self and to the TAS of others, too. Remember, shadows and darkness are light distanced in awareness from itself. Shining light offers a form of remembering and a beacon for self and others to return to the light as the love we truly are. Contrast can serve as leverage, not as a hindrance. Contrast can propel curiosity, creativity, and conscious awareness, and thus it serves as a springboard for change.

Current configuration of conscious expression. Current reality constructs; our current state of being; our experience of ourselves as we presently perceive *the way things are.* Our configuration can be either rigid, where things do not appear to change, or in flow, where change happens naturally.

Decoherence. A non-unitary process that describes a thermodynamically irreversible disturbance in the state of the environment by the system, in contrast to a distortion of the system by its environment. When a system interacts with its environment, decoherence gives the appearance of wave-function collapse, which prevents elements in the quantum superposition of the system and the environment's wave function from interfering with each other.[4] Decoherence is the expression of distinction, stemming from indistinct coherence.

In interactive reality-creation, choice is expressed through decoherence. From a coherent field of undifferentiated potential, our choice decohered from the all and expresses as a single, unfolding reality. (*See also* Coherence)

Desires. Inner sensations of curiosity that propel us to take action in a certain direction. When listened to, True Authentic Desires (TAD) that well up from the field of the heart spark a creative impulse that leads us to experience the unfolding of our true magnificence. (*See also* True Authentic Desires)

170

Disease (dis-ease). A state of being that describes a lack of ease and flow within the interconnected systems of the individual body hologram. In this state of being, symptoms of disease are often clustered together and labeled as a diagnosis. Classified in terms of diagnoses, diseases are engineered morphic fields. (*See also* Wellness)

Distinction memes. Arbitrary delineations made by labeling and categorizing reality.

Doing nothing. *Do nothing and leave nothing undone* is the core of what we teach our students to do for themselves in ME. When we do nothing, we gain access to the all that is consciousness potential. When we do nothing and get out of the way, that is, when we are *not* the doer, we become an open door for grace to enter and work through us.

Done. At a transformative level, *done* refers to the state in which the patterns we were entangled with that prevented us from loving unconditionally have been released. Done does not necessarily mean we are done interacting with a pattern altogether. There are many levels of done and each offer us a different prism of awareness.

It is done before we have begun and done is never really done in a state of flow. How we choose to engage with our own awareness relative to being done with a pattern is always a matter of choice.

Drop down, place intent, and let go. Guiding principles taught in ME to facilitate awareness and recognition of change: *Drop down* into the field of the heart (*see* Chapter 5 for suggestions on how to do this instantly). *Place intent*: Pick any two points that capture your attention. Where awareness goes, information flows. While engaging initially with the Two Point, intention is useful for learning to notice what we notice and then notice what is different. Intention is also in-the-tent-of-the-one. *Let go* and get out of the way so that the field of consciousness potential can express through you. It also means letting go of all expectations relating to the outcome.

Ego (Energy Going Out). A powerful tool for expression when it follows as an extension of the heart. Our True Authentic Self (TAS) invites us to accept ego and invites ego to follow as the heart leads us into manifesting the desires that consciousness is continually creating. In all endeavors, our TAS first lives from the heart and then integrates ego as a useful expression of universal consciousness. When we embrace ego as an extension of us, it simply *is* as a part of our continual unfolding. When we perceive ego as something to destroy or control, then the idea of ego is still seeking to destroy itself. The more we battle ego, the more we are enslaved by the idea of ego. Constructs can constrict us. But, when constructs are integrated, they can liberate us.

Electromagnetic field of the heart. According to research conducted at the Institute of HeartMath:

> The heart generates the body's most powerful and most extensive rhythmic electromagnetic field. Compared to the electromagnetic field produced by the brain, the electrical component of the heart's field is about 60 times greater in amplitude and permeates every cell in the body. The magnetic component is approximately 5000 times stronger than the brain's magnetic field and can be detected several feet away from the body using sensitive magnetometers.[5]

Elevator process (E-love-ator). Process for dropping into the field of the heart. Visualize an elevator. See a miniature version of yourself stepping into the elevator and allow the doors to close. Press the Down button. Follow your awareness as the elevator descends out of your head, down through your throat, and even further down into your chest cavity. Allow the elevator doors to open. Notice what you notice when you step out of the elevator into that space of no space and no place.

Empathy. As defined by *Merriam-Webster:*

Understanding, being aware of, being sensitive to, and experiencing the feelings, thoughts, and experience of another of either the past or present without having the feelings, thoughts, and experience fully communicated in an objective manner; also: the capacity for this.

Energy. We do not know what energy is. We know what energy does. Energy is defined in the dictionary as the ability or capacity to do work.[6]

Energy work. Doing work on ourselves as work. How tiring!

Ether (also Aether). A kind of superconductive fluid that flows right through all physical objects. The ether vacuum is an extremely dense, nonetheless frictionless, medium.

Explanation. A set of statements that make something clear or easy to understand. Also, the act or process of telling, showing, or being the reason for or cause of something. Any explanation uses language to articulate something that language cannot adequately explain. Explanations are simply bridges for our individual awareness to comprehend something that transcends explanation. Words as carrier waves convey what we perceive might be happening, not what is *actually* happening. We can never know with absolute certainty what is *actually* happening. The moment we decide that we know with certainty what is happening, we actually limit what we can access. Remember, concepts and explanations serve as maps to describe the territory of consciousness, but they are not the territory itself.

Exponents of grace. When coupled with components of grace, a component of the field of the heart can be amplified or multiplied. This component of the heart field can be expressed as a mathematical equation for accessing personal power wherein the Heart Field × Grace = Exponential Personal Power (HF × G = EPP). As with any mathematical equation, the components of grace can extend in multiple directions. Any component of personal power, when divided by grace, can summate and consummate the various functions of the field of the heart. They are interrelated, interconnected, interdependent, symbiotic, synergistic, synchronistic, tessared, and torsioned.

FanTAStic. The experience of discovering, embodying and experiencing True Authentic Self (TAS). This experience is also noticed in True Authentic Relating (TAR) and when manifesting True Authentic Desires (TAD). Experiencing fanTAStic is not fantasy. It is a joyful new reality of you *in relation to* . . . everything!

Fear. Love in a confused state.

Field of the heart. The field of the heart provides us with direct access to our inner voice, our inner wisdom, and our inner chamber of limitless potential. (*See* Heart field)

Grace. The expression of the unconditional love that is universal consciousness.

Heart-centered awareness. A state that naturally enables us to transcend the perceived limitations of duality, polarity, and contrast. There is nothing to do, and *nothing* to compare. Heart-centered awareness taps into a well of limitless information and energetic potential. It embodies the space of all-inclusion and personal power because it evokes the knowledge that there is nothing over which to exert power.

Heart field. A space of no place that provides us with direct access to our inner voice, our inner wisdom, and our inner chamber of limitless potential. Dropping down into the heart field enables us to embody a coherent state of awareness, thus bypassing the segregation and limitations of the mind to access the totality of consciousness before the collapse of the wave function. In the heart field, we go directly to the sea of coherent potential. We tap into consciousness potential by connecting to the most authentic part of us, which knows itself as whole, limitless, timeless, and dimensionless. We leverage coherence within a unified field when we drop into heart-centered awareness. There is no *doing* from that state of heart-centered being. It is an altered state of consciousness; when embodied, it becomes a vehicle for a new reality based in unity, love, and limitless potential.

The heart field is not the actual physical heart but includes the physical heart because the heart field is all-inclusive. The heart field is shaped like a double or tube torus, which are also referred to as torsion fields.

Holographic universe. Theoretical physicist David Bohm concluded that the reason subatomic particles are able to remain in contact with one another, regardless of the distance separating them, is not because they are sending some sort of mysterious signal back and forth; it is because their separateness is an illusion. Bohm postulates that the ultimate nature of physical reality is not a collection of separate objects, as it appears to us; rather, physical reality is an undivided whole in perpetual, dynamic flux.

For Bohm, the insights of quantum mechanics and relativity theory point to a universe in which all parts merge into one totality. This undivided whole is not static; it is in a constant state of flow and change. It is invisible, a kind of ether from which all things arise and into which all things eventually dissolve. Indeed, even mind and matter are united. Bohm refers to his theory as the holomovement. The terms *holo* and *movement* refer to two fundamental features of reality. *Movement* refers to its constant state of flux; *holo* signifies that reality is structured in a manner similar to holography. Bohm states that the universe is like a hologram.

Hologram. According to American author Michael Talbot:

> A hologram is a three-dimensional photograph made with the aid of a laser. To make a hologram, the object to be

photographed is first bathed in the light of a laser beam. Then a second laser beam is bounced off the reflected light of the first and the resulting interference pattern (the area where the two laser beams commingle) is captured on film. When the film is developed, it looks like a meaningless swirl of light and dark lines. But as soon as the developed film is illuminated by another laser beam, a three-dimensional image of the original object appears. The three-dimensionality of such images is not the only remarkable characteristic of holograms. If a hologram of a rose is cut in half and then illuminated by a laser, each half will still be found to contain the entire image of the rose. Indeed, even if the halves are divided again, each snippet of film will always be found to contain a smaller but intact version of the original image. Unlike normal photographs, every part of a hologram contains all the information possessed by the whole.

Holon. A morphic unit. The term was coined by Dr. Rupert Sheldrake. (*See also* Morphic unit)

"How is this useful?" Question that allows curiosity to engage with a pattern in an open-ended, non-judgmental way.

Impersonal. Not personal, as in void of personal perspective, individuation, or human emotion. Includes all perspectives as an extension of being inherently without perspective. Consciousness potential, like unconditional love, is impersonal.[7]

Implosion physics. Physicist Daniel Winter's scientific model, in which he concludes that the entire material universe is created from one non-material substance, the ether.

Individual, Individuality. Our uniqueness. Individual (in-divide-u-all) and individuality (in-divine-duality) refer to our unique experience of ourselves, not as separate and apart from universal consciousness, but as direct extensions of it. We are all unique expressions of universal consciousness, and we all stem from that which includes all identity.

Infinite potential. Unlimited possibilities and expressions; without limits or boundaries.

Information (inform-in-action). Information, as potential, is stored within consciousness containers known as torsion fields. Information resonance establishes a connection to the information, activating its potential, and what is expressed is energy and experience.

Informational field. A morphic field of information as potential. (*See also* Morphic field)

Integrity. Integrity is authenticity. Nothing to fear. Integrity is not some external standard that is incessantly beyond reach, or a mark that we will miss akin to SIN which is: Separate, Identify and Name. Integrity is within us, and is not something to earn. Like grace, it is freely available if we choose. Integrity is simply being wholly (who we truly are) without identifying ourselves exclusively through the masks and personas that we may hide behind. Authenticity is not so scary. Many spend their whole lives running from themselves and hiding inherent greatness behind projections. Waking up to being exactly who we are, with total acceptance, can stop the exhausting marathon of avoidance. In the pause, if only for a moment, there is a meeting of the soul as our unique sole signature begins to express in an entirely new and liberated way. It becomes like breathing. Easy. Integrity, as authenticity, brings forth joy from within. Nothing to do other than to be. Integrate (In-to-great), and express from that natural whole state.

Integrity is also the expression of coherence and congruence in all intentions and actions. Integrity is a presence of heart and mind that responds honestly in the moment to *what is* with full transparency. We make a powerful choice when we embrace integrity. When we embody integrity, coherence invariably follows, as they are not mutually exclusive. Integrity establishes a coherent field of connection with all that is, allowing for all that we already are to unfold into all that we are meant to become.

Intention (In-tension). Intention is to release all tension, interest, and resistance to what is to create a currency for flow as change. Simply choose, notice, let go, trust, allow, and choose. Intention, in ME is defined as *In-the-tent-of the-one,* which, to me, means to connect to all that is through unity. To me intention is opportunity, as a portal to unity.

Joy. An ever-present essence that is found through the heart's inherent connection to universal consciousness. Joy is available to us regardless of our circumstances. Joy is our natural state of being. When we embody a present state of joy consistently, joy shimmers, a brilliant translucence in the intersecting waves of our reality.

Knowingness. Knowing without knowing how we really know; trust as a timeless transformative treasure. Heart-centered awareness is a knowing without knowing how we know. This knowingness expands our awareness from a prison of limited intellect to a prism of intuitive, inherent, and infinite intelligence. Knowing now without knowing how we know; to know, to choose, and to experience from the field of the heart is the presence of knowingness. The inherent ability to access universal consciousness, and infinite potential.

Left brain. The logical part of the brain that compartmentalizes and segregates information. This part of our awareness separates, identifies, and names. The linear, logical part of the brain is a *serial processor* that can track only a few bits of information at a time. The left brain collapses the wave function; its perception is limited to seeing exactly what it expects to see. (*See also* Right brain)

"Let go into the gap and notice that the gap is no longer there." When our heart's desire and its outward manifestation are similar, the gap between them is no longer there. The gap can be a placeholder in our awareness, marking our progress and movement toward desired experience. Awareness of the gap can be a marker for consciousness, showing us that, because we are in perpetual motion, we are never stuck. When we let go into the gap, we create a bridge from our heart's desire to its manifestation, and then we notice what we notice as we traverse the bridge that spans the two.

Letting go. Also known as surrendering or allowing. Allowing provides for a return to flow. When we allow for change, which is our natural essence, then change becomes an allowance for unlimited potential. Letting go is a liberation of attachments to *what is* and *what seemingly is not.* Letting go is an embrace with the all-inclusive; it embraces everything. Inclusion is freedom that has no opposite. It simply *is* and *is not,* together, as one. When we allow, embrace, and include everything, we have no need to hang on to anything.

Leverage. A trajectory or marker in our awareness allowing for personal evolution, transformation, or coherence within a unified field so we may witness the unfolding of something different. (*See also* Wiggle room)

Limiting memes. Patterns of information that may prevent us from accessing our full potential. We can identify these memes and replace them with more useful, more expansive memes. Several categories of memes are universal in nature and either hinder us or help us gain access to our full consciousness potential. Parental, intellectual, emotional, social, relational, and survival memes often limit us. Examples of limiting memes include but are not limited to

> Not good enough
> Don't deserve
> Programmed to recreate problems
> Programmed for pain, sickness, disease
> Programmed not to accept help
> Programmed for guilt

(*See also* Useful memes)

Love. Love is All. All is Love. Love IS. (*See also* All)

Manipulation. Twisting love and siphoning it off into a constrictive funnel called *agenda.* Clear the agenda. Love is free of agenda. Manipulation is a method of using love to suck power. Manipulation creates a power struggle and a drain on our resources.

Maps. Models that explain consciousness. Maps expand our experience of ourselves as limitless beings. Maps are tools for navigating through all the patterns of consciousness. Remember, however: the maps are not the territory.

Mask. A form of projection we habitually wear when relating to others and also to ourselves. Masks are a choice, not a must. Most people, though, are not aware that their masks are not who they are. Masks do not ultimately define us or limit us, unless we let them. Any representation of ourselves that is not who we truly are in our essence is a mask.

Some masks are useful personas that help us navigate effectively through experiential reality, especially *in relation to* others. Masks limit us when we identify with them, that is, when we think the mask is who we are instead of simply a chosen container of consciousness expression we step into that extends from our true self as no-self to that which is the all. When a mask becomes a permanent fixture of our self-projected awareness, we may lose sight of who we truly are.

All masks are constructs. Masks by themselves are not inherently good or bad. Some masks are useful, and some are not so useful. Being able to notice our masks while retaining the essence of our True Authentic Self is the difference between experiencing rigidity, limitations, confusion, and dis-ease vs. leveraging masks for greater flexibility, expansion, clarity, and well-being.

Matrix Energetics. A powerful morphic field of consciousness potential that provides for instantaneous and lifelong transformation of physical, mental, emotional, spiritual, relational, financial, environmental, and self-referential patterns. Based upon widely known principles of quantum physics and lesser-known principles of torsion physics, ME taps into a morphic field of infinite potential and provides easy access to limitless possibilities.

Miracle. Any occurrence that is outside the realm of expectation or beyond preconceived notions of what is likely to occur. When we let go of expectations, preconceived notions, and attachment to specific outcomes, then every moment is a miracle unfolding. When we expect the unexpected, the unexpected soon becomes the new normal. Miracles are consciousness potential unfolding through us, as us.

Morphic field. A term coined by biologist Rupert Sheldrake in his *Hypothesis of Morphic Resonance*. It is a field within and around a morphic unit that organizes its characteristic structure and pattern of activity. Morphic fields underlie the form and behavior of holons, or morphic units, at all levels of complexity. The term *morphic field* includes morphogenetic, behavioral, social, cultural, and mental fields. Morphic fields are shaped and stabilized by morphic resonance from previous similar morphic units, which were under the influence of fields of the same kind. They consequently contain a kind of cumulative memory and tend to become increasingly habitual.

Morphic resonance. As defined by Rupert Sheldrake:

> The influence of previous structures of activity on subsequent similar structures of activity organized by morphic fields. Through morphic resonance, formative causal influences pass through or across both space and time, and these influences are assumed not to fall off with distance in space or time, but they come only from the past. The greater the degree of similarity, the greater the influence of morphic resonance. In general, morphic units closely

181

resemble themselves in the past and are subject to self-resonance from their own past states.[8]

Morphic unit. According to Sheldrake:

A unit of form or organization, such as an atom, molecule, crystal, cell, plant, animal, pattern of instinctive behavior, social group, element of culture, ecosystem, planet, planetary system, or galaxy. Morphic units are organized in nested hierarchies of units within units: a crystal, for example, contains molecules, which contain atoms, which contain electrons and nuclei, which contain nuclear particles, which contain quarks.[9]

Meme. Richard Brodie, in *Virus of the Mind*, defines a meme as "a unit of information in a mind whose existence influences events such that more copies of itself get created in other minds."[10] He looks at memes in terms of their "catchiness" and defines the effectiveness of a meme based on how quickly the thought is replicated.

Neutrality. The state in which there is no charge on the positive or negative polarity. There is also no judgment. *What is* just *is* in its entirety. Both sides of the polarity, positive and negative, are included. Neutral resides in the space between positive and negative, and that is where things most readily change. Neutrality is all-inclusive. Neutrality (new-to-our-reality) does not mean not caring; it means feeling connected to everything, which means that everything is available. Neutrality creates an opportunity (portal-to-unity) for us to transcend our perceived limitations. Neutrality is an extension of oneness and provides us with the leverage for something to change. When we relate to one another, being neutral is a compassionate form of caring.

Nodal point. A standing wave pattern. Every experience we have ever had is encoded as a nodal point in our personal hologram. According to physicists:

The wave pattern associated with the natural frequencies of an object is characterized by points that appear to be standing still. For this reason, the pattern is often called a "standing wave pattern." The points in the pattern that are standing still are referred to as nodal points or nodal positions. These positions occur as the result of the destructive interference of incident and reflected waves.[11]

Noticing what is different, not what is the same. A method for moving awareness into resonance with change that is *already* happening. We tend to notice what is not changing, which usually serves to reinforce things as they are.

Not knowing. We can access our full potential when we move beyond perspectives of what we think we know. Rigid adherence to ideas and beliefs about anything creates limiting parameters, shrouding us from expanding into the realm of indeterminacy, where all things are possible.

By opening into not knowing, we gain access to everything that extends beyond the inkling of what we know. From an expansive space of not knowing, our awareness moves from a limited perspective into that which is without perspective and limitless. Knowing nothing provides access to all.

One. All. Love IS. One is universal consciousness, expressing from consciousness potential or unconditional love, which can be represented by zero. *One* is part of *Zero* and contains all of Zero, but One is not greater than Zero. From Zero, as *no-thing,* comes *something,* and that *something* is One. Unconditional love (Zero-point field as consciousness potential) that expresses as One may be considered *conditional* or *conditioned* by virtue of the parameters it has chosen. The parameters chosen are One. Just One. However, since One is all-inclusive, there are really no boundaries. *All-inclusive* means infinite inclusion, infinite expansion, infinite possibilities, and infinite expression. Thus, One is still unconditional love.

Opening our lens of awareness. Refers to expanding our personal, limited perspective beyond the confines of our thoughts, opinions, beliefs, and perceptual biases to include the realm of not knowing. By resonating in a space of not knowing, we gain access to everything that falls outside the limited parameters of what we think we know. As a result, we access more possibilities from the realm of the infinite.

O-port-unity. Opportunity and a portal to unity.

Parallel universes or many worlds interpretation (MWI). From mathematician and quantum theorist Hugh Everett III, these terms refer to a model of quantum physics that seeks to explain what happens outside the collapse of the wave function. The theory postulates that a wave function collapse may never actually fully occur. The theory states that there is a *universal wave function,* and that every possibility that can occur does occur. All possibilities become actualities, albeit in alternate realities.[12]

Parallel Universe process. A method taught in ME for expanding references and resonance with other aspects of ourselves, beyond what we are noticing and experiencing now. Because we can expand our personal resonance utilizing Parallel Universes, we are able to experience ourselves differently; we are able to easily and consistently tap into multiple options that are extensions of consciousness to actually experience ourselves as the multifaceted, limitless beings that we truly are.

Pattern. Information contained in a specific configuration, which, through resonance, is expressed as energy and experience. Our experience of reality is a result of our resonance with patterns of information. Labeling a problem as a pattern allows us to move our awareness into neutral territory. Furthermore, it provides us with wiggle room to reconfigure the pattern. Interacting with a *pattern,* rather than a *problem, condition,* or *disease,* also frees that pattern from its morphic and memetic resonance with other similar patterns. (*See also* Placeholder)

Pebble dropping into a pond. A metaphor to describe our perceived personal reality. The pebble represents our choices. The pond represents universal consciousness. Choosing to drop a pebble into the pond creates a ripple effect that emanates in all directions, reverberating through everything related to your choice. The pebble creates the ripples. In turn, the ripples respond to our pebble. (*See also* Ripple effect)

Perfectly imperfect. Describes the experience of the True Authentic Self (TAS); the experience of existing peacefully within oneself as a limitless being with perceived limitations. It is totally perfect to be perfectly imperfect. (*See also* True Authentic Self)

Personal power. A function of grace, personal power is not power over anything or anyone. As defined in this book, personal power is power that comes from direct access to the field of the heart and from the infinite potential that is available when we plug into the grid of universal consciousness potential. A heart-centered connection is not about having power over anyone or anything.

Perspective. A single point of reference.

Physics of heart-centered awareness. Torsion field physics that support action at a distance, remote healing, instantaneous healing, time-travel, levitation, invisibility, and unlimited (free) energy. The physics of torsion fields is an emerging model that seems to explain what has been going on for thousands of years. It is the physics of us. It is the physics of love.

Placeholder. A pattern of information in our external reality construct that reflects back to us a piece of ourselves that we have yet to recognize from within. We may perceive placeholder patterns as problems, diseases, relationships, or anything we resonate with that is an aspect of our personal-perspective reality. (*See also* Pattern)

Play. A state of being that has no agenda but to joyfully engage with the moment and notice what we notice. Play puts us in our hearts and enables us to bypass our linear, logical, analytical brain, which constructs our reality based on what is familiar. Play is the portal to freedom of choice; it offers the ability to respond to our circumstances instead of reacting. PLAY is Potential Love Awaiting You to join in the fun. Choose to play. Just play!

Possibility states. The transient unfoldings of our limitless potential *prior to* its actualization as experience. Possibility states surround us in every moment.

Practicality. The state of being practical, as applied to the aspects of a situation that involves the actual doing or being experience of something, rather than theories or ideas about it.

Practically perfect. The practice of being and experiencing what already is perfect. Practically perfect does not mean *almost perfect* or *not quite perfect*. Practically perfect is the practice of recognizing the inherent perfection in everything.

Practical play. M-Joy approach to everything that is universal consciousness. Everything is practical. Everything is play.

Problem. Defined by *Merriam-Webster* as "a matter or situation regarded as unwelcome or harmful and needing to be dealt with and overcome." This predominantly negative personal perception sees certain matters as being in our way, which limits our options. On a polarity scale, a problem gets a negative charge. The unknown solution for an identified problem would sit on the opposite end of the polarity scale, yielding a corresponding positive charge. Unfortunately, as long as we are attempting to focus on finding a solution for a problem, we are resonating with its polarity, and that is the problem.

Projection. We may come to know ourselves through the reflections of others. When these reflections from others are not accurate, we can forget who we truly are. When these reflections are projections of distorted perceptions, we may encode information that does not match our limitless essence.

Protection. Defense against perceived harm or loss. When we are in a reality subset that says we need protection, we can know that our perception needs protection, too. As long as we *believe* we need protection, we need protection. The perceived need for protection is a matter of resonant vibration. Where we resonate, so we shall experience. Love needs no protection. Awareness of love is protection. Sometimes love wears a raincoat or camouflage to get through a storm or jungle. Awareness is key. Protection is simply an extension of awareness. If you perceive a need for protection, see yourself inside a pink bubble of unconditional love and invite that bubble to expand to include everything you notice.

Questions. Questions are the answer. The answers are within the questions.

Reality. We can never definitively know what reality is. We can know reality only through how we perceive it. Our lens of awareness provides us with a mechanism for noticing, perceiving, and experiencing something we call reality.

Reality-creation. The process of actively participating with universal consciousness to create and manifest experiences.

Relating. A dynamic, ever-evolving essential of relationships. Relating describes us *in relation to*. Relating is us *in relation to* universal consciousness and its infinite potential. Relating is us *in relation to*—everything!

Resonance. Vibration.

Right brain. The intuitive part of our brain. The right brain is a parallel processor that is able to track multiple waves of possibilities simultaneously. The right brain can track patterns of information as probabilities *before* they are actualized. The language of the right brain is symbolic and pattern-oriented. It can track connections that typically are not captured by the segregating, serial processing of the left brain. The right brain appears to be governed by waves of interconnecting grids of possibilities. It is able to follow many waves *prior to* their becoming droplets of choice in the sand.

When we expand our awareness into a state of playfulness that has no expectation, agenda, or attachment to an outcome, when we expand it beyond what we expect to see and beyond thinking, then we enter into the domain of right brain awareness. By perceiving via the intuitive right brain, we are able to readily *uncollapse* the wave function into various possibility waves that await our further recognition. (*See also* Left brain)

Ripple effect. Refers to the inherent connectivity of everything. In the earlier metaphor about dropping a pebble into a pond, the pebble represents your choices. Wherever you drop a choice into the pond of universal consciousness, it creates ever-expanding ripples that spread in all directions, reverberating through everything directly or indirectly related to your choice. The ripple effect also applies to transformation and love. The ripples of universal consciousness respond to your choices. The ripple effect is the holographic placeholder for your interactive reality-creation. The ripple effect applies to everything that is related to you. (*See also* Pebble dropping into a pond)

Search. Awareness expressing through our curiosity, synchronized with infinite potential.

Secondary gain. Motivator, conscious or unconscious. Within strategy memes and association memes, often there are secondary gains with which we resonate either consciously or, more likely, unconsciously. Continuing to run a program or hang onto a pattern may be due to a secondary gain. Remove the secondary gain and the pattern often falls away.

Selfish and *Self-is*. Loving self is not selfish. Our True Authentic Self (TAS) knows this truth. Rather, we might call it *self-is*, because the TAS recognizes self as a direct extension of universal consciousness. Moreover, self-care is a potent carrier wave for joy. Appreciating ourselves honors our needs and desires in myriad ways. It amplifies love, and more love becomes available for others. There is nothing selfish in loving self.

Spirituality. Spirituality means something different to everyone. Many define spirituality as the search for something sacred outside the domain of the physical world. As defined in this book, spirituality is practicality, and practicality is flexibility of consciousness. Flexibility of consciousness is a portal to freedom.

Strategy memes. Ideas or beliefs that relate to cause and effect. Strategy memes help us navigate from point A to point B. When we take certain steps, we will experience a certain outcome. Strategy memes are extremely useful for organizing consciousness in a predictable way that facilitates accomplishing specific goals.

Sympathy. An affinity between people or things in which they affect each other. An inclination to think or feel like another. Energetically, sympathy is entraining oneself to another's resonant vibration. Practically speaking, when another is miserable and we sympathize, we are likely to become miserable, too.

Synchronicity. According to Carl Jung, "Synchronicity is the coming together of inner and outer events in a way that cannot be explained by cause and effect and that is meaningful to the observer."[13] When we are aware of synchronicity, we notice the inter-connected patterns in everything and recognize that there is no such thing as coincidence.

Tenets of Matrix Energetics. Absorb what is useful. Discard the classical mess. No way as way. These mean notice what you notice, jettison the limitations of prior training and self-limiting perceptual biases, and get out of the way so the field can flow through you to express what occurs spontaneously in the moment.

Time. According to *Merriam-Webster Dictionary,* "a nonspatial continuum that is measured in terms of events which succeed one another from past through present to the future."

Time as torsion. In 1913, Dr. Eli Cartan was the first to demonstrate clearly that, in Einstein's general theory of relativity, the flow of space and time not only *curves* but also possesses a spinning or spiraling movement within itself. This is known as torsion.[14] It is generally accepted that the space surrounding the earth, and perhaps the entire galaxy, has what is called *right-handed spin.* This simply means that energy is influenced to spin clockwise as it travels through a physical vacuum. This torsion research was expanded by the work of Nikolai A. Kozyrev in Russia. Using rotation and vibration in laboratory experiments, systematic research was able to demonstrate that it is torsion fields that influence the flow of time.[15]

Time Travel process in Matrix Energetics. An effective strategy for releasing limiting patterns from the past and to expand into resonance with limitless potential.

Torsion. Spin.

Torsion Field. The quantum spin of empty space, the large scale coherent effects of the spin of the particles in the virtual sea. Torsion fields appear to be everywhere in the universe and are forms of subtle energy. A torsion field is also known as a *spin* or *field, axion field, spin field,* and *microelectron field.* In the 1920s, Albert Einstein and Elie Cartan did initial work in this area of study, which is now known as the ECT (Einstein-Cartan Theory). On a macroscopic level, torsion fields are generated by classical spin or by the angular-momentum density of any spinning object. The spinning of an object sets up polarization in two spatial cones, corresponding to a left torsion field and a right torsion field. At an atomic level, nuclear spin, as well as full atomic movements, may be the source of torsion fields, which would mean that all objects in nature generate their own torsion fields. These fields are not affected by distance; they instantaneously spread out through space; they interact with material objects by exchanging information; and they explain such phenomena as telepathy and photokinesis.

Torsion-field physics. An emerging model of science that studies torsion fields. It is also known as scalar physics.

Torus. A unique form of flow in hydrodynamics, a torus allows fluids to spiral inwards and outwards on the same surface of the torus. It is a very stable flow form. If the universe is essentially created from one universal substance, the ether, it must be form that is used to create different and separate things out of this universal substance. The torus is nature's perfect-flow form for creating in the formless ether a seemingly separate entity that is stable enough to last. Everything is formed through the torus. The heart field is a torus. The torus is the container through which consciousness expresses itself as matter, form, and experience.

Transactional interpretation of quantum mechanics (TIQM). A theory proposed in 1986 by John G. Cramer at the University of Washington. This model explores quantum interactions of time in terms of the following: A standing wave that travels forward in time is referred to as a *retarded wave*; a standing wave that travels backward in time is referred to as an *advanced wave*. Where the waves intersect, a cancellation occurs, creating the present moment. Cramer claimed there is really no observer effect or collapse of the wave function, but rather that time is an ongoing flow of intersecting standing waves. This work implies that time is bidirectional, not unidirectional. Cramer also did some pilot research with photons and demonstrated that photons could travel backward and forward in time.[16]

Transcend (trance-end). To rise above or go beyond, overpass, or exceed is the general meaning. In this book, to transcend means to move beyond a limited construct of consciousness into a new form of information expression, energy, and experience.

Transcending (trance-ending) duality. The experience of recognizing that duality is part of our experience but does not limit our experience. This is also referred to as unity consciousness.

Transform (trance-form). To modify the form or expression of something. Our essence as limitless beings is a constant that does not change. Our experience or expression of that essence is the process of change experienced through transformation.

True Authentic Beauty (TAB). Inner radiance that wells up from the field of the heart and shines throughout the physical body temple. Translucent brilliance of TAS that is a unique expression of universal consciousness and infinite potential. No comparision. Only completion.

True Authentic Desire (TAD). Genuine desires that well up from the field of the heart. True Authentic Desire is a cue from universal consciousness to pay attention, for when allowed to unfold, TAD manifests as magnificence. TAD's are feeling states that are not characterized necessarily by emotions or logic. Rather, they are an inner knowing. TAD is a knowing what we know without knowing how we know. TAD can be most readily accessed and expressed when embodying True Authentic Self (TAS) and in True Authentic Relating (TAR).

True Authentic Opinion (TAO). Perspective expressed honestly in the moment. TAO can be most readily accessed and expressed when embodying True Authentic Self (TAS) and in True Authentic Relating (TAR).

True Authentic Power (TAP). Inner strength and truth accessible through the field of the heart and grace. Nothing to power over. Inner dominion.

True Authentic Relating (TAR). The congruent expression of coherency by our True Authentic Self. True Authentic Relating is integrity-in-action. TAR is clear intent and right relations.

True Authentic Self (TAS). Differs from our authentic self, which embodies limitations. Our TAS embodies limitlessness with limitations. In effect, it says, "I know I am consciousness potential and a being without limits, and yet I coexist peacefully with my self-imposed limitations. Daily, in each moment, I am unfolding and letting go of who I was the moment before so that I can embrace more of who I am becoming." Our TAS has presence and awareness of divine being, which is unconditional love in the form of coherent light. It also has limiting self-concepts that have been conditioned into personal awareness. These co-exist and synthesize without judgment. Our TAS is willing to explore parts of the self that may not match the picture of its limitless being, opening into those parts with the same love and light. Our TAS embraces the full totality of being; it does not hide the yucky stuff from awareness. Our TAS is perfectly imperfect.

TAS commitment vows. Our most important intimate relationship is the one we have with ourselves. It is you *in relation to* you, an eternal marriage between your true authentic self and your heart. The vows are simple, profound, and meaningful. Commit to love, honor, and listen to yourself through your heart, in sickness and in health, for richer or poorer, in death you won't part. Vow to appreciate, encourage, and support yourself when you need it most, and even when you do not need it. Promise to always be honest with yourself and to express your truth as it occurs to you. When you forget any of these promises, remember the premise of forgiveness, as forgiveness is an ever-evolving gift of grace. Find your joy in this marriage with yourself. Be joy. Live joy. In-Joy! Love self first and foremost, and from there, love exponentially. Love is the ripple effect.

Truth. Ultimately, truth is a deeply personal experience. For the purposes of this book, truth means understanding our own truth for ourselves in regard to the nature of our own reality as a limitless being.

Two (too!). Everything *in relation to* . . . Everything is you, as One, *in relation to* an other. In relation is Two.

Two Point. A construct developed by Dr. Richard Bartlett, founder of ME, the Two Point is a method of engaging in an ongoing conversation with universal consciousness. The method leverages awareness to expand beyond resonance with what we are currently noticing or experiencing so that we may witness the unfolding of something different. The Two Point method allows us to connect *what is* with what we desire to experience. The Two Point is an ongoing dance with universal consciousness in which we may easily move awareness from where we perceive ourselves to be and into the transformation we seek to embody as experience. The Two Point enables our individual awareness to move from dual points of perspective into the all, which is pointless, without perspective, and without distinctions. The Two Point moves awareness beyond duality into the unity that is universal consciousness with its infinite potential.

Unconditional love. The cohesive force that unifies all, as well as that which creates the fabric of the universe. Unconditional love is not the kind of love that we humans have become accustomed to, with all its parameters, expectations, and limitations. It is not "I love you." It is Love IS. Expressions of love, no longer unconditioned by virtue of being conditioned into an expression, are powerful, coherent placeholders for our potential return to wholeness and connection with Source as universal consciousness.

Universal consciousness. As defined in this book, universal consciousness is the mechanism for everything, and in fact *is* everything. Universal consciousness is all. The essence of universal consciousness has been described as spirit, light, love, nature, torsion, and ether. It has also been described as who we are. In other words, we don't just experience universal consciousness; rather, universal consciousness *is*, and it experiences itself through us. (*See also* All)

Unity consciousness. The state in which oneness and duality are perceived as an extension of unity. Duality is part of our experience but does not limit or define our experience. (*See also* Trance-ending duality)

Useful memes. Patterns of information that assist us in accessing our full potential. Examples of useful memes include but are not limited to

> Will to create
> Will to accept
> Will to love
> Will to learn
> Will to change
> Will to forgive

(*See also* Limiting memes)

Vibration. Resonance.

Vortex. A little eddy or tornado that draws everything that surrounds it into its powerful current.

Wellness. A natural flow that is expressed through a body of information that serves as a vehicle for consciousness. Thus, wellness, or well-being, is a conditioned expression of consciousness and love flowing through form from its original unconditional state. Ultimately, well-being is consciousness potential expressing itself as love and light through us. Focusing on well-being without trying to be well or to avoid disease allows our natural state of flow to well up and reverberate from the core of our being. When we let go, we are in flow. Wellness or well-being is a matter of conditioning consciousness. Condition yourself to be free from your conditions. Energetically align awareness to focus upon where you want to be, so that form and function may follow.

Whole. The essence of that which we are. Complete. There is no hole in whole.

Wiggle Room. Leverage. Information noticed within a pattern that offers the greatest degree of flexibility to unravel a pattern and create a different configuration. A perceived opening into a different possibility, noticed beyond the current experience. Movement of awareness through a rigid construct to create greater flexibility, expansion and flow. Wiggle room is what we notice, or perceive, when interacting with patterns that have been defined as problems, conditions, or disease. Wiggle room can be identified by asking an open-ended question such as, "If I knew where the *wiggle room* is within this pattern, so that the pattern could change, what might I notice?"

x **axis.** In a Cartesian coordinate system that makes use of graphs to plot coordinates on an *x* and *y* axis. As defined in this book, a *0,0* point on the *xy* axis, or the zero-coordinate point, represents us in our present resonance. This is our zero-point reference for the present moment and is the coordinate that represents here and now. In this construct, moving awareness along the *x*-axis represents time travel, which provides us with flexibility of consciousness that moves horizontally in time.

y **axis.** In a Cartesian coordinate system as described above, the *y*-axis represents parallel universes, which provide us with flexibility of consciousness that moves vertically across universes.

You. Everything. All. I AM. Love. Universal consciousness and its infinite potential.

Zero. A placeholder with infinite value. For example, the placeholder Zero represents unconditional love as consciousness potential. Zero is *not* nothing, as in *without value*. Zero is *no-thing*, whole and all-inclusive of all values or expressions. Zero is perhaps empty space full of potential. As no-thing, Zero has no parameters and no perspective. It is a Zero-point field of infinite consciousness potential.

Zero-point energy (aka Zero-point field). Quantum science in the twentieth century revealed the presence of an all-pervasive background sea of quantum energy in the universe. Cambridge University's Dr. Harold Puthoff was one of the first to measure this energy. He measured it at zero degrees Kelvin, the absolute lowest possible temperature in the universe, which is equal to minus 273 degrees Celsius. According to Newtonian physics, at this temperature all molecular and atomic movement should have ceased that is, no energy should be measured at all!

Instead of finding no energy, as expected, Dr. Puthoff found what he called "a seething cauldron" of energy; henceforth, it was given the name Zero-point energy (ZPE). Puthoff proved that the physical vacuum is not at all devoid of energy and that, instead of being a vacuum, space is actually a plenum.

Princeton University's John Wheeler and Richard Feynman were the first to value the zero-point energy. They calculated that a cup of Zero-point energy is enough to bring all the oceans of the world to the boiling point. Contrary to what we have always believed, matter is not a condensed substance but a diffuse form of energy.

The field of the heart gives us direct access to the Zero-point field. The Zero-point field is also considered consciousness potential.

Notes

Chapter 2

1. Institute for Applied Biophoton Sciences, http://www.biontology.com.
2. Swanson, "Life Force: The Scientific Basis," 43.
3. Ibid.
4. Ibid.
5. Hammond, "Torsion Power."
6. McKenna, "New Maps of Hyperspace."
7. http://www.dark-side-of-the-rainbow.com.
8. http://www.in5d.com/carl-jung-synchronicity.html.
9. Ibid.

Chapter 3

1. http://www.sheldrake.org/research/glossary.
2. Sheldrake, *Morphic Resonance*.
3. http://www.sheldrake.org/research/glossary.
4. Ibid.
5. Dawkins, *The Selfish Gene*.
6. Principia Cybernetica Web, http://cleamc11.vub.ac.be.
7. Dawkins, *The Selfish Gene*, 192.
8. Brodie, *Virus of the Mind*, 11.
9. Ibid., 19–23.
10. Ibid., 20.
11. Ibid., 21.
12. Ibid., 23.
13. Open CRS, "Direct-to-Consumer Advertising of Prescription Drugs."

Chapter 4

1. http://www.rense.com/general69/holoff.htm; see also Talbot, *Holographic Universe*.
2. Bohm, *Wholeness and the Implicate Order*.
3. http://www.rense.com/general69/holoff.htm.
4. http://www.sheldrake.org.
5. http://www.sheldrake.org/Resources/faq/answers.html.

Chapter 5

1. http://www.divinecosmos.com.
2. Institute of HeartMath, "The HeartMath Definition."

3. *Waking Times,* "Heart Has Its Own 'Brain' and Consciousness."
4. Wicherink, "Aether Vibrations."
5. Ibid.
6. Ibid.
7. Ibid.
8. Ibid.
9. Ibid.
10. http://www.iop.org/news/13/mar/page_59670.html.
11. Swanson, *Life Force: The Scientific Basis,* 524.
12. http://www.difoet.heerfordt.dk/net/1/1-2.pdf.
13. Hammond, "Torsion Power."

Chapter 7

1. Jones, "Does Time Really Exist?"
2. Cramer, "Transactional Interpretation of Quantum Mechanics."
3. http://www.crystalinks.com/holographic.html; see also Talbot, *Holographic Universe*.
4. Physics Classroom, "Standing Wave Patterns."
5. International Metaphysical University, "Torsion Fields and the Science of Time."
6. Ibid.

Chapter 8

1. Everett, "Theory of the Universal Wave Function."
2. http://physics.about.com/od/quantumphysics/f/manyworldsinterpretation.htm.

Chapter 9

1. Hershey, "Coherent Heart: A Discussion with Dr. Rollin McCarty."
2. Institute of HeartMath, "The HeartMath Definition."

Chapter 10

1. Green, "Jesus on Science," 341.

Chapter 11

1. Brodie, Virus of the Mind, 23.
2. Institute for Applied Biophoton Sciences, http://www.biontology.com.
3. Institute of HeartMath, "The HeartMath Definition."
4. Joos et al., Decoherence and the Appearance of a Classical World in Quantum Theory.

5. Waking Times, "Heart Has Its Own 'Brain' and Consciousness."

6. http://umdberg.pbworks.com/f/energysummary.pdf.

7. Wicherink, "Aether Vibrations."

8. http://www.sheldrake.org/Resources/glossary/index.html.

9. Ibid.

10. Brodie, Virus of the Mind, 11.

11. Physics Classroom, "Standing Wave Patterns."

12. Everett, "Theory of the Universal Wave Function."

13. http://www.in5d.com/carl-jung-synchronicity.html.

14. International Metaphysical University, "Torsion Fields and the Science of Time."

15. Ibid.

16. Cramer, "Transactional Interpretation of Quantum Mechanics."

Bibliography

Bischof, Marco. "Biophotons: The Light in Our Cells." *Journal of Optometric Phototherapy*, March 2005, 1–5.

Bohm, David. *Wholeness and the Implicate Order*. London: Routledge, 2002.

Brodie, Richard. *Virus of the Mind: The New Science of the Meme*. Carlsbad, CA: Hay House, 2009.

Cramer, John G., and the American Institute of Physics. "The Transactional Interpretation of Quantum Mechanics." *Reviews of Modern Physics* 58 (1986): 647–88.

Dawkins, Richard. *The Selfish Gene*. Oxford: Oxford University Press, 1976.

Everett, Hugh, III. "The Theory of the Universal Wave Function." http://www.physics.about.com.

Green, Glenda. "Jesus on Science." In *Love without End, Jesus Speaks*, 2nd rev. ed. Sedona, AZ: Spiritis, 1999.

Hammond, Richard T. "Torsion Power." Unpublished manuscript, North Dakota State University. http://gravityresearchfoundation.org/pdf/awarded/1996/hammond.pdf.

Hershey, Stephen. "The Coherent Heart: A Discussion with Dr. Rollin McCarty." *Reality Sandwich Blog*, 2012. http://realitysandwich.com/130470/the_coherent_heart.

Institute for Applied Biophoton Sciences. http://www.biontology.com.

Institute of HeartMath. "The HeartMath Definition." http://www.heartmath.org/templates/ihm/e-newsletter/publication/2012/spring/heartmath-definition.php.

International Metaphysical University. "Torsion Fields and the Science of Time." http://intermetu.com/2012/03/torsion-fields-and-the-science-of-time.

Jones, Andrew Zimmerman. "Does Time Really Exist?" http://physics.about.com/od/timetravel/f/doestimeexist.htm.

Joos, Eric, H. Dieter Zeh, Claus Kiefer, Domenico J. W. Giulini, Joachim Kupsch, and Ion-Olimpiu Stamatescu. *Decoherence and the Appearance of a Classical World in Quantum Theory*. 2nd ed. New York: Springer, 2003.

Jung, Carl. *Synchronicity: An Acausal Connecting Principle*. Vol. 8 of *The Collected Works of C. G. Jung*. Princeton, NJ: Princeton University Press, 2010.

BIBLIOGRAPHY

McKenna, Terence. "New Maps of Hyperspace." In *The Archaic Revival: Speculations on Psychedelic Mushrooms, the Amazon, Virtual Reality, UFOs, Evolution, Shamanism, the Rebirth of the Goddess, and the End of History*. New York: HarperCollins, 1992.

Miller, George A. *Psychology: The Science of Mental Life*. New ed. New York: Penguin Books, 1991. First published 1962 by Harper and Row.

Nin, Anaïs. *D. H. Lawrence: An Unprofessional Study*. Paris: Edward W. Titus, 1932.

Open CRS. "Direct-to-Consumer Advertising of Prescription Drugs." Congressional Service Reports for the People. May 20, 2009. https://opencrs.com.

Physics Classroom. "Standing Wave Patterns." http://www.physicsclassroom.com/class/sound/Lesson-4/Standing-Wave-Patterns.

Principia Cybernetica Web. http://cleamc11.vub.ac.be.

Sheldrake, Rupert. *Morphic Resonance*. South Paris, ME: Park Street Press, 1995.

Swanson, Claude. *Life Force: The Scientific Basis*. Tucson, AZ: Poseidia Press, 2011.

———. "The Torsion Field and the Aura." *Subtle Energies and Energy Medicine* 19, no. 3 (2008): 43–89.

Talbot, Michael. "Does Objective Reality Exist?" http://www.rense.com/general69/holo.htm.

———. *The Holographic Universe*. New York: Harper Perennial, 1992.

Vesperman, Gary. "Torsion Field Physics and Communications." http://www.padrak.com/vesperman/Torsion_Field_Physics_and_Communications.doc.

Waking Times. "The Heart Has Its Own 'Brain' and Consciousness." September 2012. http://www.wakingtimes.com/2012/09/12/the-heart-has-its-own-brain-and-consciousness/.

Wicherink, Jan. "Aether Vibrations." In *Souls of Distortion Awakening*. http://www.soulsofdistortion.nl/SODA_chapter6.html.

Winter, Daniel. "Implosion Physics: The Real Grail Is in Your DNA." http://www.soulsofdistortion.nl/Dan%20Winter.html.

About the Author

Melissa Joy is best known for her ability to engage people from all over the world to embrace their true authentic power through accessing universal consciousness by playing in the field of the heart. She has a unique perspective on how we are able to experience living joyfully, and loving completely from a state of grace.

Melissa Joy has been teaching ME life transformational seminars around the globe since 2008. She is also the founder and instructor of the 'M-Joy Of Being' seminar series, a unifying movement in consciousness dedicated to exploring and expanding heart-centered awareness and practical personal empowerment.

She is sought after as a respected published author, as well as a frequent guest speaker on global radio broadcasts. She is well known for her eloquent articulation, and personable accessibility on both nationally and internationally recognized social media platforms.

Melissa Joy is passionate about inspiring others to realize their True Authentic Self (TAS) with practical, creative, and powerful wisdom that she embodies every day. She enjoys long runs near the ocean, reading, walking barefoot in the sand, and sharing with people the joyful journey of living their infinite potential.

Printed in Great Britain
by Amazon.co.uk, Ltd.,
Marston Gate.